CHRISSIE HYNDE

AMERICAN MUSIC SERIES

David Menconi, Editor

CHRISSIE HYNDE

A MUSICAL BIOGRAPHY

ADAM SOBSEY

UNIVERSITY OF TEXAS PRESS ⋎ AUSTIN

Requests for permission to reproduce material
from this work should be sent to:
    Permissions
    University of Texas Press
    P.O. Box 7819
    Austin, TX 78713-7819
    http://utpress.utexas.edu/index.php/rp-form

♾ The paper used in this book meets the minimum
requirements of ANSI/NISO Z39.48-1992 (R1997)
(Permanence of Paper).

LIBRARY OF CONGRESS CATALOGING-IN-
PUBLICATION DATA

Names: Sobsey, Adam, author.
Title: Chrissie Hynde : a musical biography /
    Adam Sobsey.
Other titles: American music series (Austin, Tex.)
Description: Austin : University of Texas Press,
    2017. | Series: American music series
Identifiers: LCCN 2016033834 | ISBN 9781477310397
    (cloth : alk. paper) | ISBN 9781477313312 (library
    e-book) | ISBN 9781477313329 (nonlibrary e-book)
Subjects: LCSH: Hynde, Chrissie. | Rock musi-
    cians—United States—Biography. | Pretenders
    (Musical group)
Classification: LCC ML420.H9976 S63 2017 |
    DDC 782.42166092 [B] —dc23
LC record available at https://lccn.loc.gov/2016033834

doi:10.7560/310397

For Heather, tough and tender

CONTENTS

INTRODUCTION

"Just don't buy the fucking book, then, if I've offended someone," she said in 2015, in an interview to promote her new book, a memoir called *Reckless*. She'd sooner lose the sale—and fans—than her integrity. Even if it gives offense, she stands by her truth, which in *Reckless* was all of four words: *I take full responsibility*.

This is why people love Chrissie Hynde. They love her even if they haven't heard a note she's written or sung, in that instantly recognizable voice of hers, since she had her last hit, more than twenty years ago. And most people haven't. They love her despite knowing virtually nothing about her or her band, the Pretenders. In a world full of pretenders, Chrissie Hynde is unassailably authentic, and it's her authenticity that gathers and unifies the details of her life, that makes it possible to adore her without really knowing them.

She is probably America's foremost woman rocker: an icon in eyeliner, a voice for the ages, and a great (and greatly underrated) songwriter. She is "the greatest female singer, maybe ever," as one eminent music impresario put it,[1] and her greatness is steadfast and unchanging. She looks the same, sounds the same, and swears

1

the same as she did when she and her band burst out of London's punk scene in the late seventies, and there has never been anyone quite like her. She's a self-possessed, self-exiled idol with no real forebears; a complete original who, despite trailblazing for countless female musicians, has always disdained the idea of "women in rock" and has no true musical descendants.

Yet as self-contained and singular as she is, as thoroughly herself, Chrissie Hynde is full of contradictions, and she can be hard to apprehend. "Every time I try to get close to you, you throw nails in the road," she sings on the 1999 Pretenders album ¡Viva El Amor! That lament could just as easily be sung about her. She's a Hindu and a vegetarian who has gotten herself arrested protesting animal rights, but she has defended the death penalty on religious grounds. Her songs have featured plentiful and strong sexual content, and her most famous song is about using her body to attract attention, yet she has virtually never presented herself as a sex object, and she sharply criticizes women rockers who do. She's a generous, charismatic, entertaining live performer who is frequently prickly and combative with her fans, the public, and the press. After half her original band died young of drug overdoses, she made the most accomplished album of her career without them.

She's the very image of snarling rock-chick toughness, but she writes and sings tenderly, tremulously about the vulnerabilities of love and motherhood; she may be the only significant woman in rock to make motherhood itself an abiding musical subject. She had romances with two high-profile pop stars, but she has mostly lived singly, quietly, and plainly in London, where she raised her two daughters far from the spotlight, taking eight years off from touring to be a mom at the height of her career. She's an American treasure who has lived nearly her entire adult life in London. She's a Hall of Famer, a musical force for four decades, but she has made only eleven studio albums.

Chrissie Hynde seems, then, not so much divided as double, as if there is both a Chrissie: the voice, the persona, the rock goddess, and a Hynde: the songwriter, the mother, the Hindu. (It's for this reason that I've found it comfortable, throughout this book, to refer to her as neither Chrissie nor Hynde, or sometimes as both.) As she sings—or warns, or even boasts—on a late Pretenders album, "I'm a very, very complex person."

Chrissie Hynde's complexities and contradictions are not only the key to her enduring appeal, they're also why she is worthy of a book. Yet her own memoir, *Reckless*, doesn't really do them, or her, justice, and its author inadvertently explained why shortly after it was published: "The stuff I really regret, I left out of the book."[2] She left out much more than her regrets. For one thing, the narrative of *Reckless* ends in 1983, leaving more than thirty years of her life and career untouched. For another, her book often repeats familiar stories she and her cohort have been telling publicly for years. The events these stories recount are now several decades old, and many of her recollections are drug-clouded, so *Reckless* is twice unreliable. Thrice, really: an assiduously protective type, she takes care throughout the book to be circumspect about the actions and motives of her intimates. Her omissions are sometimes quite conspicuous. The ex post facto controversy over *I take full responsibility* was far more charged and provocative than anything in *Reckless*, which, despite its title, is anything but. The memoir is best read not as a historical document but as a Chrissie Hynde album, a retrospective anthology of mostly well-known songs, occasionally interspersed with an early track or neglected rarity. Its most valuable moments are Chrissie Hynde's terse but clear philosophical aphorisms, which give clues to what has driven her actions over the years. (All of the unattributed quotations in this book are from *Reckless*.)

The most important missing element in *Reckless* is, glaringly, Chrissie Hynde's music. What inspired it, how it was made, what it might mean to her—none of this is in her memoir. Her music is as closely guarded as her children, and it's naturally where my attention turns in this book: this is largely a *musical* biography, less

concerned with seeking the singer in her songs than with study-
ing the work of an artist whose music spans nearly four decades
and more musical genres, from punk to pop, country to chamber,
blues to bossa nova. To that end, I make occasional brief detours
into musical analysis. The composer's use of chords, modulations,
and meter are sometimes jarringly unpredictable or deceptively
complex, like Chrissie Hynde's character and actions—and also
like her famous voice, which is actually "two different voices: one
for the ballads and one for the rockers."[3] These unpredictabilities
and complexities are nearly always strongly linked to the lyrics,
stories, and moods of her songs. I have tried to maintain the same
connection in my technical discussions of her compositions.

You may find that this book ends somewhat abruptly—in the
middle of the road, to borrow the title of one of the Pretenders'
hit songs—and in fact right where it began, with Chrissie Hynde
snarling, "Don't buy the fucking book." That is deliberate, and not
only for the practical reason that she is very much alive and kicking, and almost surely has more music in her. (Indeed she does,
announcing a new Pretenders album as this book was in production.) The controversy over *Reckless* was simply her last salient act
before I concluded.

The book's ending-as-beginning and avoidance of finality are
also motivated by its subject's spirituality. In her early adulthood,
Chrissie Hynde was introduced to the ancient Hindu scriptural
poem the *Bhagavad Gita*, and she has been devoted to it ever since:
it is "the glory I bask in," she calls it in *Reckless*. Anyone who wants
to understand her would do well to read the *Bhagavad Gita* and to
consider the fittingly contradictory character and circumstances
of its protagonist, Arjuna. He is a warrior who, on the brink of
battle, suddenly does not want to fight. He gives halt orders to his
charioteer—who at once reveals himself to be the god Krishna and
who, for the rest of the poem, sermonizes to Arjuna not only on
the dilemma at hand but, more important, on the nature of being.
Over and over, Krishna touches on notions of impermanence, the

incompleteness of the self, and the endless cycle of all life into and out of death.

What will last is the music. "She will always carry on," Chrissie Hynde sings in "Hymn to Her." "Something is lost, and something is found." She would probably appreciate that although she sang that line, she didn't write it. ("The self is not the doer," the *Bhagavad Gita* counsels.) "Hymn to Her" was composed by Meg Keene, one of her childhood friends, and she gave it a voice as an interpreter. This book, this hymn to her, is offered in the same spirit of interpretation, with the modest hope that in it something of Chrissie Hynde may be found.

ONE

TALK OF THE TOWN
Beginnings

We would assume our "horse" personas on the playground. . . .
I was Royal Miss, a chestnut mare with two white stockings and
a star on my forehead.

— *RECKLESS*

A spirit animal. A star on her forehead. White stockings.

White-gold ankle boots glow from the foreground of the picture on the cover of Chrissie Hynde's memoir, *Reckless*. The rest of her is in black and white. The long, wild mane falls over her shoulders. Her bangs hang low, obscuring the star on her forehead. She has always worn them long. She never wanted fame. She just wanted music. She wanted to be as close as she could get to it, and to the people who played it.

Chippewa Lake Park, Cleveland. September 2, 1966. She was about to turn fifteen. She went with some friends to hear Mitch Ryder and the Detroit Wheels play. This was when bands still regularly performed at amusement parks and fairgrounds, under tents. It was an afternoon gig. The Wheels' guitarist, Jim McCarty, dazzled her. She was dazzled again when a fight broke out among the band and aborted the set. She persuaded her friends to stay for the evening show. Another fight broke out; it was staged. Real rock and roll was actually part pretending. She thought, "That's got to be the life!"[1]

Less than a year later she went to a Jackie Wilson show in Cleveland. He spotted her in the front row and called her up on stage. She was mortified. Then he kissed her—it was her first kiss. To be loved by Jackie Wilson!

But let's examine this moment more closely. Jackie Wilson was well known for his "kiss lines." These were "fairly orderly" processions, as one recollection put it: girls and women in the audience would line up; Jackie would splay out over the lip of the stage and kiss them, one by one, booze and mouthwash on his breath.[2] The kiss was real, but the situation was pretend—and she put herself right in the front row for it, her star near the light.

Later in high school, she went to see the Paul Butterfield Blues Band. Before the show, "My friends and I inadvertently wandered into the backstage area while looking for our balcony seats," she writes in *Reckless*, "and straight into Paul Butterfield himself." (Inadvertently? And are balconies usually near backstage areas?) She got Butterfield's autograph.

A year or so later, early in 1968, she and her friend Cindy drove to Cleveland from Akron, where she grew up, to see the Jeff Beck Group in concert. She and Cindy often drove up to Cleveland to go to shows, stoned, but this was different. Jeff Beck was one of her biggest rock and roll heroes. Cindy knew a DJ who had what was needed for access to the band: "a baggie full of killer weed."[3] The girls were the paraphernalia. They tried to look as British as they could. Soon they were in a hotel room with Rod Stewart, who was Jeff Beck's singer; Ron Wood, who was Jeff Beck's bassist; and Brian Jones, the Rolling Stone, who was just hanging around—and who would soon be dead, joining the 27 Club with Jimi, Jim, and Janis. She wouldn't even form her band until she was twenty-seven.

In *Reckless* she writes: Stewart "grabbed a guitar off one of the twin beds, wielding it like a pool cue, and rammed the headstock into my bony rear end. But sexual innuendo was lost on me." Drugs were not. She got very stoned in the hotel room, but she soon understood that Cindy was going to pair off with Brian Jones and that she herself was going to go with Ron Wood and lose her virginity to him.

Even though she was out of her mind and in over her head, she was somehow still quick on her feet. She seems to have always had a canny, high-alert, hair-trigger instinct, no matter the situation. A few years later, while she was a student at Kent State University, she earned credits by participating in a psychology department experiment. "I was instructed to press a button every time a certain image came up on a screen. The guy conducting the test raised his eyebrows and told me that I had the fastest reaction times of any woman they'd tested on campus."

She told Ron Wood that she had to go and take the driver's license exam first thing in the morning, and she fled with a disappointed Cindy in tow. How exactly they escaped is unclear, since by her own account Jeff Beck had taken the keys to Cindy's Corvette and gone for a joyride. Five years later, Cindy went with her to London.

In 1970, she drove through a blizzard to hear the Kinks play in Pittsburgh. Ray Davies was another one of her heroes. After the show, she was outside the venue on the sidewalk when who should walk past but Ray Davies himself. (Had she been waiting for him there?) They made eye contact; it was like the first exchange of cards in a very long game.

September 22, 1972, two weeks after she turned twenty-one, six years to the month after the Detroit Wheels punch-up at Chippewa Lake Park, she was working as a waitress. It was the date of David Bowie's first ever American concert, which happened to be in Cleveland: that great, underrated rock city, the future home of the Rock and Roll Hall of Fame, which inducted the Pretenders thirty-three years later. Chrissie Hynde learned her music there. She borrowed her mother's Oldsmobile and drove herself and a friend up from Akron, but not just for Bowie's show. They got there long before, in the cold gray afternoon, stood outside Cleveland Music Hall, and listened to the sound check. Afterward, the band emerged from the auditorium: Ziggy Stardust and the Spiders from Mars in a Cleveland parking lot. She and her friend approached. Confidence is a bluff, she writes in her memoirs—twice.

Soon enough, they were in a hotel room with the band. No offer of drugs this time, or of sex, but she did give the rock star a piece of advice: tonight, she said, you should play that Velvet Underground song, "Waiting for My Man." The band had more immediate concerns: they were hungry. Did she know a good place to eat? She drove them to dinner in her mother's Oldsmobile. "This is a nice car," Ziggy said, politely, in full dress and makeup in the backseat. The Olds was real, and so was the hunger, but David Bowie was pretending. That night, they played "Waiting for My Man."

She was born Christine Ellen Hynde in Akron, Ohio, on September 7, 1951. She had one sibling, an older brother named Terry who also became a musician. He's been playing saxophone in the same Ohio band for nearly fifty years. Their father, an ex-Marine, had moved them around a bit when she was very young, but they'd settled in Akron, where he worked for the phone company. Her mother was a secretary, but also a former model, with "a striking flair for color and design," as Dolores Hynde's 2012 obituary put it.[4] Christy—sometimes Chris, not yet Chrissie—came by her own flair honestly. She sewed designs on her own clothes and her friends' to wear to rock shows. Later she went to art school at Kent State University, and one of her first jobs in London was with an architecture firm.

In her childhood she dreamed of riding horses in the English countryside, but she scarcely learned to ride. When she went to England in her early twenties it was not to the country but to teeming London, and not for horses. "I was always in love with England, even as a child, because I thought everyone rode horses here," she once said. "Then I heard English music, and that was it."

She couldn't have been born at a more perfect time for English music. She was a teenager from 1964 to 1969 and insists to this day that "I grew up when all the best music happened. Every day was like Christmas."[5] The first album she ever bought was the Beatles' debut album, which came out when she was twelve. She also loved American music: R&B singers like James Brown and Sam Cooke—whose version of the Platters' "The Great Pretender" gave her band its name. She also loved Bob Dylan and Neil Young; her favorite singer was Tim Buckley. Later she had a daughter with the king Kink; later still, her band opened for the Stones. Neil Young inducted her into the Rock and Roll Hall of Fame, and when they were both past sixty he played guitar on her first solo album.

As a teenager she took up ukulele, not guitar. Eventually her parents bought her a guitar, but her first role in a band was as a singer with a group called Sat Sun Mat. She didn't last long. She was too shy—so shy that in order to bring herself to sing she had to take the mike on a long cord and shut herself in the laundry room, where no one could see her. Fifteen years later, when the Pretenders made the album *Learning to Crawl*, the rest of the band had to leave the studio while she recorded the vocals with only the producer and engineer present.

One of her bandmates in Sat Sun Mat was a high school classmate named Mark Mothersbaugh, who later formed the band Devo. Devo's debut album was produced by Brian Eno five years after she interviewed Eno for London's *New Musical Express*, where she had a writing gig in the early seventies. Nearly forty years later, in 2008, she moved back to Akron and played a concert there with Devo.

But in the early seventies, all she wanted was to get out. Many Akronites wanted out of Akron, but not as far as she wanted out. They were in white flight to the suburbs. The subsequent urban disintegration pained her; she loved cities, especially hers. But the driving hurt worse. "I wanted to get out of cars," she said. "I could see the way car culture was going."[6] She didn't just want out of Akron; she wanted out of America.

This vehement rejection of cars, which she has often expressed, seems disproportionate to her radical choice to leave the United States, but it's as authentic and unique to Chrissie Hynde as her legendary singing voice. Car culture put all of her aversions into one vehicle. She grew up walking. She'd walk for hours with her girl-hood friend, all the way into and around downtown Akron. People would be out and about, moving and mingling. She and her friend would go to the department store lunch counter and share a grilled cheese: this was prelapsarian urban life, when the hearts of cities still beat strong. If you had to get somewhere faster than you could on foot, you could take the train. The lonesome whistle called to her, and called her away. "Since I was in junior high school, and this train used to go by, I know it sounds romantic, but it made me cry when I saw it. I just knew that I had to be on that train someday."[7] She'd never really get off the train, and she'd never entirely leave home. When she was sixty-three, she told an interviewer, "I'm still writing about Akron and I'm still writing about trains."[8]

In Akron, in America, they were paving over everything. Car culture overran both the city—"reduced to parking spaces," she'd sing years later, in "My City Was Gone"—and the country: "My pretty countryside had been replaced by shopping malls." Cars accompany, in fact require, the twin destruction of the best of human civilization and the glory of nature, and Chrissie Hynde was uncommonly sensitive to the destruction of nature. In her teens she embraced vegetarianism when it was still a fringe practice of the counterculture, especially in the Midwest. The death of cities worsened segregation, too. "This is no place for me," she sings fretfully about Cleveland in "Pack It Up," on *Pretenders II*. More than a quarter century later, in 2008, she'd call for the destruction of Cleveland's Innerbelt, and all the roads, with the Pretenders' album title: *Break Up the Concrete*.

Break Up the Concrete's final song is a sweetly nostalgic tune called "One Thing Never Changed":

> *That old train keeps blowing*
> *Through the center of this town*
> *Restores my faith*
> *When the chips are down.*

She keeps the faith even though "it don't take no passengers since the streets got rearranged" to accommodate all that traffic, which Americans have so completely joined that they've almost literally become their own cars:

People come and go
Like cars changing lanes
But that whistle's gonna blow
Because one thing never changed.

When the Pretenders were inducted into the Hall of Fame in 2005, she ended her speech with "two notes: Keep moving. Never change."[9] Just like the train.

She graduated from high school undistinguished and unambitious, and enrolled at Kent State, where there were signs of hope: a downtown train, people who walked around, like-minded vegetarians, and a thriving campus counterculture at the height of the Vietnam War. If she had had any ambition at all to be a visual artist—she did have some talent—she might have had a very different career. But drugs had defrayed what little drive and self-discipline she had, and the signs of hope at Kent State were destroyed by the infamous shootings in 1970, which happened within her earshot. "Four dead in O-hi-o," sang her hero Neil Young.

She left Kent State, moved back to Akron, and began to gather material for the first Pretenders album, although she couldn't have known it at the time. She started hanging out with the "Heavy Bikers"—her term for the Hell's Angels she'd first encountered as security detail at rock shows. One day she took Quaaludes and went up to Cleveland to visit an ex-boyfriend in jail, where there were some Heavy Bikers dropping in on one of their own. She got acquainted with them on the elevator down and accompanied them back to their lair, where they sexually assaulted her. "I roll with the punches," she said, years later. "I don't get traumatized."[10]

The assault became the basis for the Pretenders song "Tattooed

Love Boys." It also became a formative moment in establishing her fascination with the Biker, an archetype who has ruled over her life and art with a dark, enduring, almost godlike power. "Like a tattoo or a dog," she writes in *Reckless*, "the Heavy Bikers were for life." They were for music, too: the Pretenders were formed from a vision she had of "Motorcycles with Guitars." Decades later she composed a paean called "Biker" for the 1999 Pretenders album *¡Viva El Amor!* It was never released as a single and isn't well known, but she was still featuring it in her live sets as late as 2014.

Meanwhile she was waiting tables and doing more and more drugs. Yet she always had a deeper, cannier instinct—that presence of mind that summoned awareness of her driver's license exam at exactly the right moment and enabled her escape from Ron Wood. Despite the drugginess of its account, *Reckless* seems to gain authority and validity as it goes on. Its author's plain-spoken directness of tone, the abiding Midwestern pragmatism at the reins of her recklessness, her sheer persistence, her bona fides as a rock Hall of Famer: all of this makes her hard to doubt or deny, even when her choices and opinions seem wrongheaded or demonstrably errant.

When she declares that she grew up at the very best time for rock music and names all the legendary bands that were in their heyday during her adolescence, objection seems laughably pedantic. When she justifies her vegetarianism with the simplest, most elemental logic—"Why would anyone kill an animal if they didn't need to?"—meat-eating suddenly seems not just bloody and grotesque but also a witless, pointless waste of energy: "Every intelligent person," she declares, "will eventually become a vegetarian."[11] When she argues, against the social tide, that it's a bad idea for a scantily dressed, heavily drugged young woman to accompany Hell's Angels wearing "I Heart Rape" badges back to their lair ("that's just common sense"), it's hard to argue without politicizing the issue. About her decision to have a baby, she explains simply, almost as if it should be obvious, that a woman having as much sex as she was eventually had to accept the biological consequences.[12] "Everything in nature lives according to some order," she writes in *Reckless*—including humans, "even if they try to resist their instincts. That's how we can be sure we're not animals, this refusal to abide by what we know is good for us. If an animal's instinct tells him to avoid something, he has no trouble keeping a wide berth. We, on the other hand, run in the direction of danger if it offers a thrill or satisfies a curiosity."

After she dropped out of Kent State, she applied to the Ontario College of Art in Toronto, not because she had any strong desire to continue her studies, but because she'd liked Toronto when she'd gone up there not long before. And she wanted to see the world. Canada wasn't far, but at least it was over the border. The school accepted her, and her parents were even willing to pay her tuition. But even though Toronto was technically a country away, it wasn't far enough, and it wasn't big enough.

London was. Moving there was probably the defining act of her life. It is the place that gave her a career, a family, and a permanent home. But why London? Why not New York or Los Angeles or even Paris (where she'd wind up soon enough, for a while)? It started with the childhood dream of riding horses in the English country-side, and it continued with wanting to see the world. Then it was practical: no language barrier. And of course she was young, and young people make shallow, unconsidered decisions.

What wasn't shallow or unconsidered was her love of English music—not just English music, but what England stood for musi-cally at the time. It was the place to be, no matter what you liked to listen to. Her favorite American rocker at the time, Iggy Pop, was better loved in London than he was in the United States, or so she thought. She'd found him through his most famous fan, David Bowie. Years later, she'd name Iggy's "Five Foot One" as her ideal song. Together they'd get wasted in New York City and go up the Empire State Building and perform his hit duet "Candy." She and the Pretenders would beat Iggy and the Stooges into the Rock and Roll Hall of Fame by five years.

In the spring of 1973, twenty-one years old, she got a passport and sold her guitar to buy a plane ticket to London, where she hoped to become a rock musician. It was an O. Henry choice, it seems, to sell her musical instrument in order to make music. But the long game she was playing required occasional gambits. It even required a bit of hoping against hope: she thought it was already too late for her to be a rock musician. Anyway she wasn't much of a guitarist. "My job is to make the band sound good," she often says, and she does. It's the talent she most readily admits to.

She packed two Iggy albums and not much else, and persuaded her friend Cindy to go to London with her—the same Cindy who'd gone with her to see the Jeff Beck Group in 1968, wound up in that hotel room afterward, and then escaped with her. This time they were escaping America together and running toward English music, not away from English musicians.

Here is a one-sentence biography of Chrissie Hynde: She went to England in the seventies, formed the Pretenders, became famous, and never came back to Ohio. It's a tidy narrative, but it didn't happen that tidily, or that quickly. It took her long and far out of her way—so far that she did come back to Ohio for a while.

Immediately upon arrival in London, she fell in love with the city, the way young people fall in love with big cities when they go there for the first time. She moved all around and took different jobs, from selling handbags in an outdoor market to working for a couple of architects—her Kent State art studies helped her land that gig. But she only kept it for a few months. She'd moved to London for music, not architecture. "I thought if I kept not doing what I didn't want to do," she writes in *Reckless*, "I would naturally get close to what I did want."

She began to get closer. When she took Iggy's albums with her to England, she had left a photo of him hanging on her wall back home in Akron. The photo accompanied an article about Iggy in *New Musical Express* magazine, which she read religiously (a record store owner in Akron stocked it, surprisingly). One night in

London she was at a party where someone said he knew Iggy. He turned out to be the guy who had written the *NME* article. It also turned out that he needed a place to stay, so she let him stay with her. More than stay: he soon dumped all of his things at her place. "The guy moved in on me!"

The guy was Nick Kent. We know him now as a legendary rock journalist, but in 1974 he was one of those scenesters—part writer, part rocker, fully connected—who attach themselves to the zeitgeist. Kent got her some writing assignments for *NME*, including her interview with Brian Eno (and also a starstruck one with Tim Buckley). Eno told her about "this new Japanese thing," which referred not to any music but rather to his shaved pubic hair, along with his admiration for Nippon pornography. When the interview was over, Eno dressed her in some of his bondage gear. Photos of the two of them appeared in the article, as did their shared judgment: "We conclude that art which demands participation holds the greatest appeal." Even in the early guise of a professional music journalist, she seemed eager to dress for the rock life itself—to be a participant, not an observer.

Her Eno interview and her other articles for *NME* were published under the byline "Chrissie Hynd." Nick Kent had given her a new name to go with her new job. He also gave her a couple of STDs and, thanks to a nasty breakup row, a permanent scar on her hand. She dumped him and reclaimed the E for her last name, but she was never known as Christy again. (In his memoir, *Apathy for the Devil*, Kent disputes most of her account of their relationship, although not the STDs.) She soon dumped *NME*, too. Her first assignment had been to write about a new Neil Diamond album— a sign of the musical times. She slaughtered it. That got her some attention, but not the kind she wanted, especially not when she "became 'Chrissie Hynd of the *NME*,' which I really didn't like."[13]

She came to regard her music journalism as regrettable at best. Toward the end of 1974, she was asked to do a retrospective on the Velvet Underground. She'd been a fan since at least "Waiting for

My Man" (she'd brought a third album with her from Ohio to London along with those two Iggy and the Stooges records: the Velvet Underground's *White Light/White Heat*), but she was appalled by the assignment: "I thought, 'Why always looking back?' Working in this shop seems so much more happening than looking back at the past, so I left."[14] She sold her typewriter to another rock journalist, Julie Barnhill, and began working exclusively at "this shop," another job Nick Kent had gotten her.

"This shop" was a place called Sex, Malcolm McLaren and Vivienne Westwood's now-legendary punk fashion boutique. She loved it. "The great thing about their clothes was that they were doing everything that was the antithesis of fashion. It really appealed to me because it was saturated with all these Virgo qualities, all this attention to detail. I began walking round wearing all this stuff, like a rubber skirt, fishnet stockings, and these high-heeled shoes. It was the first shop where I thought, 'I can wear this gear exclusively, and never go to another store.'"[15] It wasn't just the clothes she liked, though. She liked talking with McLaren about music and where it was going—that wasn't quite clear yet, but it was coming from Sex, the teapot from which punk's tempest sprang. Sid Vicious and Steve Jones, half of the future Sex Pistols, sometimes hung around the shop.

But "the job didn't last long":

One day we were just closing up—Malcolm was there—and Nick Kent came into the shop. He thought I had been seeing someone else, so he took off this belt he was wearing, which had big coins on it, real cheap and nasty, and started whipping me with it. I hit the floor then ran into the dressing room and Malcolm hid underneath the counter. I still have a tiny scar. The next day, Malcolm said, "It's too confusing you working here." So I went to three record companies a few days later, got about forty albums, sold them and got a ticket to Paris.[16]

Another O. Henry moment: she used London music to get her out of London music. As "Chrissie Hynd of the *NME*" she could still requisition promo copies of records, which she sold for a plane ride. She'd met a Parisian in London who wanted her to be in his band, but when she got to Paris, she discovered that he had no band. She stayed in Paris anyway, in a flat with the other singer in this nonband, along with the singer's transvestite lover and their dog. They got stoned and ate brown rice together and read deeply in the *Bhagavad Gita*, the ancient Hindu philosophical poem. She hung around Montparnasse and had an Afghani-cum-cowboy-gambler boyfriend. Although nothing much happened for her career in Paris, the time was deeply formative: happy, spirit-filling, self-discovering.

But she didn't stay in Paris, either. No band was forming, her visa was expiring, she had no money and no prospects, and Paris was in the throes of a heroin epidemic. That was the one drug she wasn't interested in. Early in 1975, the girl from Ohio who exiled herself to London, became a Pretender, and never went back to Ohio, went back to Ohio. "When you start to get serious," she writes in *Reckless*, "your roots become everything."

Those roots were actually quite healthy. It wouldn't be long before Ian Hunter wrote the song "Cleveland Rocks," and in 1975 the city already had punk rock of a sort, an avant-noise scene anchored by Pere Ubu and the Electric Eels, whose circle included future drum god Anton Fier and the talented, doomed guitarist Peter Laughner. She called up a guy she knew, named Duane Verh, who had wanted her to audition for his band before she left for England. He still had room for her, in an R&B cover act called Jack Rabbit. She hadn't lasted long in Paris but had started to figure out who she was; she didn't last long in Cleveland either, but she started to figure out how to sing. Jack Rabbit played in bars and clubs, where she sang Isley Brothers tunes and Jackie Moore's "Precious, Precious."

Was the seed planted for the Pretenders' "Precious," the lead track on their debut album? Certainly that song got its motor if not its title from her time in Cleveland: it's a driving tour of the city's underbelly, where much of the songwriting on side one of *Pretenders* gestated. (A hitchhiking fiasco she recounts in *Reckless* must have given her "Up the Neck.") She also started hanging out with the Heavy Bikers again, against her better judgment. She even took up with one of them romantically.

What if Jack Rabbit had worked out and she had stayed in Cleveland? Would they have become a national treasure—a Hall of Fame act? Or would she have sunk back into Ohio obscurity and worked as a waitress all her life, riding on the back of a Hell's Angel's Harley? She has sometimes said waitressing would have been her only alternative if she had failed at rock and roll. She would have spent her life asking, "Would you like sour cream on your baked potato, honey?" as she does on "Watching the Clothes," a song on the third Pretenders album. She had no other skills or ambitions in 1975. While she was in Jack Rabbit, she went back to work in a diner, as she'd later do in the Pretenders' breakthrough "Brass in Pocket" video. But music aside, Cleveland was a bad idea from the start: it was a city in deep and dangerous decline, gutted by the suburbs she so detested. Despite Jack Rabbit, she was miserable, in with a bad crowd, and constantly in trouble, if not outright peril.

She had a chance to get out. Malcolm McLaren rang her up and proposed to fly her back to London to front a band he wanted to concoct, but she declined. The act he had in mind didn't sit quite right with her. For someone who wanted to rock as badly as she did—and who, at the same time, was already worried that it was too late—she was surprisingly stubborn about what kind of band she'd consent to join. Perhaps she didn't feel ready, despite her age; she was still learning to sing, and she still wasn't much of a guitarist. But maybe the name of McLaren's proposed band stuck in her head for a song title she'd later come up with. They were to be called the Love Boys.

After the apartment building she was living in burned down, she moved in—and did drugs—with a woman named Annie, who happened to be her mother's former hairdresser. (Presumably her mother didn't know about Annie's drug habit.) She was so comfortable with Annie, and so disillusioned by Cleveland (and restless as always), that she followed her all the way to Tucson, Arizona, where Annie had decided to move. But she was just as miserable there as she had been in Cleveland. One day, she got another invitation from overseas: a telegram from a guy she'd met in Paris named Memmi, who she didn't think even knew her. He was getting a band together and wanted her to sing. This time she said yes, and he sent her a plane ticket. The next day, she was back in Paris.

The band she joined, called the Frenchies, played their first gig at the legendary Olympia Theater in Paris, but that turned out to be the highlight of their short existence. The Frenchies quickly disbanded, and this time there was no going back to Ohio again—she'd learned her lesson. Now she had a reason to stay in Europe: "I smelled something in London." That something was punk, and she knew it was for her. She left behind everything she owned in Paris and went right back to Sex.

But Sex wouldn't have her. When she returned, Vivienne Westwood called her a "despicable little piece of shit" and kicked her out of the shop without further explanation. A mutual acquaintance, John Lydon, thought Vivienne was mad at her because Vivienne had fought "over nothing in particular" with their avant-punk musician friend Judy Nylon, and "Vivienne suddenly ostracized both of them because, well, that's her thing," Lydon wrote. And "if Vivienne didn't like her . . . that was a good enough reason for me to be intrigued."[17]

They got to be friends. She got Lydon a job cleaning houses, and she got Sid Vicious a modeling job at St. Martin's College (she was making a little money at both of those things as well). She tried to interest Lydon in spirituality and the *Bhagavad Gita* (he declined) and to teach him some chords on the guitar (Malcolm McLaren declined, strenuously, on his protégé's behalf; the character he had in mind for Lydon didn't admit of guitar or Hindu scriptures).

Lydon did accept something else from her, though: a proposal of marriage. This was her idea of a permanent solution to the problem of yet another expiring visa. Had she made the proposal a bit sooner, before he became Johnny Rotten, the most infamous musician in the world, she might have become Mrs. John Lydon. But "it became obvious that he was about to be famous," she recalled. She and John took a long walk, "and he was very depressed. He was afraid his friends would change and that things would change drastically for the worst." Later, in a pub, she reminded him of the marriage plan, and he put his troubled head on the bar and moaned, "Ohhhh, Gawd!" The wedding was off. He later explained that he was just too cowardly to go through with it.

They'd have made an interesting couple: coming up together in the same London scene, both from far-off, working-class roots; two deeply musical minds, steeped in melody, temporarily disguised as punks. "If you go through John Rotten's record collection," she said, "you will find some very musical albums." And although "John's a bastard," if you take off his punk mask, "there's still something sweet and tender about him."[18] She could very nearly be talking about herself. Lydon called her "a tough old bird."[19] She called him "a compulsive liar."[20]

Sid Vicious was drinking with them when Johnny Rotten put his head down on the bar, and Sid agreed to marry her instead. A few nights later, she had Sid stay in her bed, but not to have a night-before romp with him. She just wanted to keep him close in order to make sure he'd go with her the following day and sign the papers. (Sid brought another girl to her place and shagged her instead, elbowing and kneeing his adjacent bride-to-be the whole time.) Next morning, she roused him and dragged him to the registry, but when they arrived they discovered it was closed for an extended holiday. Sid then had to go to a different government office: criminal court for some petty offense she couldn't quite recall. After that, they either forgot to go back to the registry or simply didn't bother. Curiously, her scotched marriage to a rocker, and her failure to persist in trying again, prefigured another, more important iteration that would follow years later. In 1982, she went to the courthouse with Ray Davies, but they apparently got into a row on the way, and the magistrate refused to marry them. They never went back. It seems that some plans, once foiled, can never succeed.[21]

Her near nuptials with a pair of Sex Pistols were emblematic of her near commitments to bands. She came close to joining any number of them, and did briefly connect with a few. These combos, half-formed or merely half-dreamed, tended to have meretriciously scandalous names: Big Girls' Underwear, Masters of the Backside, the Moors Murderers (who were named for a grisly serial child-murder case). After she left Masters of the Backside, they became the Damned: the first English punk group to release a single. She also offered her services as lead singer to the Stranglers, who lasted for decades.[22] But very few of the other engagements lasted even a month. Punk always lives, quite deliberately, on the verge of self-destruction.

She found some mutual interest with an all-female punk band called the Slits, but her friend Viv Albertine was a rival candidate to join them. "I'd better say yes before Chrissie moves in on them," Albertine thought to herself. "But they didn't ask Chrissie. No one wants to be in a band with her, she's too good."[23] (Imagine anyone saying that about a talented man; they would have lined up at his door to be in a band with him.)

In 1977, her friends in the Clash invited her to join them on their first British tour—but not as a member. She went along anyway. The Clash were the biggest thing going since the Sex Pistols had faded. "It was great," she said of that tour, "but my heart was breaking. I wanted to be in a band so *bad*. And to go to all the gigs, to see it so close up, to be living in it and not to have a band was devastating to me. When I left, I said, 'Thanks a lot for lettin' me come along,' and I went back and went weeping on the underground throughout London. All the people I knew in town, they were all in bands. And there I was, like the real loser, you know? Really the loser."[24]

There's a song on the 2002 Pretenders album, *Loose Screw*, called "The Losing." It was her mother's favorite song on the album:

> *The winning's not what it's all about,*
> *You see, it's about the losing.*
> *First you feel hungry,*
> *Then you're thirsty, too*
> *Then a desperate feeling comes over you.*

By 1977 that "desperate feeling" had come over her. No matter that she knew the Clash and the Sex Pistols and Malcolm McLaren. No matter that not long before punk arrived, she had been "Chrissie Hynd of the *NME*." Although "I felt instrumental,"[25] she said, she had no instrument. And she was twice an exile: from America and from the punk world that wouldn't quite accept her. She had come from Ohio and had gone to London and Paris and back to Ohio—and to Paris again and finally London again, twice retracing her steps—and all that traveling made her "a little bit too worldly," she thought, for these kids in London. Plus she was too old for them—she'd been too old to rock since 1973. In the game of musical chairs, she was the loser.

Yet what looked and felt like losing can just as easily be read, in hindsight, as winning at her own game—that much longer game she always seemed to play, no matter the field. Rather than merely joining somebody else's band (or someone's idea of one), she was determined to have her own. Even if an impresario like McLaren or his rival Bernie Rhodes or any of rock's much slimier characters, like the Runaways' rapacious Svengali Kim Fowley, had succeeded in conceiving an act for her, it's hard to imagine her ever consenting to work under anyone's thumb. Her apparent waywardness was more deeply rooted in a very clear and unwavering sense of purpose: to be the leader of her own band.

Her commitment to that dream goes a long way toward explaining why there was never any doubt who was in charge of the Pretenders once they were formed. In one of the most assured passages in *Reckless*, she writes:

> I was the boss, no messing. That was the one thing I really was good at. I always knew what was right for the music. I never doubted it. That was my main, possibly my only strong point— natural instinct.

There are echoes here of her belief that "everything in nature lives according to some order, even if they try to resist their instincts." Her instincts were so strong that she was leading her band before she even had one.

And she was getting closer to having one. She knew someone who was house painting for a well-known music entrepreneur named Tony Secunda. The painter recommended her to Secunda, and she went to Secunda's office and played him one of her songs: "The Phone Call," an angular, grating, punkish composition that didn't even have lyrics. She simply raced through the chords on her guitar "while staring him down with a defiant glare." Still, Secunda saw and heard her potential. He began paying her rent and expenses so she could quit her menial day job and write songs. When he drove her around London, he pointed at a billboard and told her she'd be on it soon. She was skeptical—not that he could get her on a billboard, but that she wanted her image on one. Fame wasn't what she was after. She just wanted to front a band. Playing in Jack Rabbit had convinced her that that was what she wanted, even if it killed her: "Like a cart horse en route to the glue factory, I just kept going."

Perhaps her only remaining asset was her familiarity with the scene from her first go-round in London. "I knew *everybody*," she said years later, almost wearily. One of the people she knew was Lemmy Kilmister of Motörhead, who were managed by Secunda.

Maybe that's how she knew him, or maybe she knew him because Lemmy had played a few gigs with the Damned when they didn't have a bassist. *Everybody* knew *everybody*. She moaned to Lemmy that she still wasn't in a band. Lemmy was an apparition of the Heavy Biker, hard and dark, and he gave her tough love. He told her to stop her sobbing: "No one said it would be easy!" But he also told her about a drummer she might want to check out. She actually wanted Lemmy's drummer, Phil Taylor, to play in her band. Taylor fit her vision of "Motorcycles with Guitars": it's almost a nonsense phrase, really, and not the actual name of the band she imagined leading, but perhaps it was a sort of sustaining dream, a projection of her rock desires. *Motorcycles with Guitars*.

She wouldn't dream of poaching Philthy Animal Taylor from Lemmy, though, and it might not have mattered even if she had tried: there were rumors Taylor would be claimed by the Heartbreakers, Johnny Thunders's band, who were in London from New York (she'd sing sloppily with Thunders at Max's Kansas City in New York just a couple of years later). The drummer Lemmy suggested she seek out had the loony name of Gas Wild, and soon after that, she happened to spot a man answering to his description from the window of the place where she was staying in Ladbroke Grove—one of countless squats, spare rooms (one vacated by a suicide), office desks, and other cramped and squalid corners where she curled herself up in London in the early and mid-seventies. She was surely drawn to Ladbroke Grove for its fertile counterculture. The neighborhood was the center of the so-called "UK underground" of the late sixties. Lemmy's first band, Hawkwind, formed there, as did Cream, T. Rex, and others. Later, the Clash got started in Ladbroke Grove; maybe the neighborhood would be propitious for her, too. But the sighting of Wild wasn't quite as lucky as it may have seemed, even though he did play drums for her briefly: he would get so drunk that he'd fall off his drum stool, so she fired him. But without Gas Wild, there might never have been the Pretenders, because it was Gas Wild who introduced her to a bassist named Pete Farndon.

Farndon was about her age—also a bit too old. He was tall, dark, and handsome, and like her he wasn't from London. He came from Hereford, a nowhere place in the west of England near Wales, known mainly for cattle and just slightly for Mott the Hoople. Being from Hereford was perhaps a bit like being from Ohio. Farndon was a seasoned veteran of numerous bands, including an Australian folk outfit called the Bushwackers (who, amazingly, are a going concern to this day). But he didn't want to stay in a folkie band whose instruments included a tin whistle and a banjo. He left Sydney, got very dissolute for a short while in Hong Kong, and then went back to Hereford, where he lived with his mum and wondered what he'd do next. That's when Gas Wild told him about this chick he was playing with in London. So Farndon went down there for an arranged meeting in a pub. "There was this American with a big mouth across the other side of the bar. She said hi, and turned around and ignored me for about an hour. I thought, 'Am I gonna be in a band with this *cunt*?'"[26]

The three of them went to "the scummiest basement" and played some songs. The first one was the R&B staple "Groove Me," by King Floyd. Farndon was intrigued. Then she taught him a couple of her originals, including a country song called "Tequila," which would not surface on a Pretenders album until twelve years after Farndon died—and then only in a one-minute snippet, a fading echo of the past. There was also "The Phone Call," the song she'd played for Tony Secunda. It impressed Farndon because it was in 7/4 time. He *was* gonna be in a band with "this cunt," and in her bed, too.

Cunt—the worst word, even allowing for its slightly milder connotation in English slang usage. Thirty years later, people were still calling her the c-word. And she was hurling it right back: "A lot of these cunts, they take credit for stuff they haven't even written. It's shameful, really, horrible."[27] The word pops up again in a comment—"fucking cunt," actually—underneath a candid-camera recording[28] of her in an airport, volubly refusing to sign an autograph hound's placard and giving him a lecture about her privacy (and then, dogmatic vegetarian as always, comparing his rapacity to that of meat eaters). It isn't the autograph request itself that bothers her; she's objecting to giving one specifically to him, making it personal. (While she's venting, she signs someone else's cardboard guitar cutout. The joke is on her: these "fans" turn out to be autograph dealers.) Once, in Los Angeles, a fan knocked on her hotel room door late at night after a show, apparently thinking an afterparty would be raging in there. "I came out with nothing on but my Iggy Pop t-shirt"—nethers exposed, imaginably—"yelling, 'How dare you wake me and my children up!'"[29] Maybe she's not the "cunt"; maybe we are, and she's just reflecting ourselves back at us.

It would be different if she were one of the male rockers whose bouts of bad attitude have strengthened rather than weakened their charisma, their complex appeal as artists. Contrary, mercurial, reticent: John Lennon could be a cunt. Bob Dylan. Her future lover Ray Davies too. But we never called them cunts, or anything so demeaning. We called them brash, or geniuses, or sometimes drunk; boys being boys, *enfants terribles*. But we seldom if ever have assailed them by their gender, which the spikiness of Chrissie Hynde's persona has little to do with. It has more to do with humor. Nearly all the best songwriters are funny, even—especially—the prickly and serious ones. Dylan, Lennon, and Davies could be quite waggish, whether "hop[ing] we passed the audition" as part of the biggest band in the world (Lennon) or calling himself "a song-and-dance man" (Dylan). Comedy softens their natural pugnacity, allows their intensity to breathe a little, and helpfully separates singers from their songs. But she doesn't seek any ironic distance; she has seldom removed that dark eyeliner. There's scarcely a playful moment in any of her songs until the wry, easygoing *Break Up the Concrete* in 2008. "She has the sense of humor of your average ayatollah," rock critic Robert Christgau wrote of her in 1987, and "her self-righteousness can be a drag."[30]

Yet this is not the complete picture, only the public one. Twenty-five years after Christgau's complaint, her close friend Morrissey wrote of her, lovingly, "She is by far the funniest person I have ever met. This is not to suggest that Chrissie *has* a sense of humor, because she doesn't appear to." His former Smiths bandmate Johnny Marr called her "really funny."[31] When she does appear to have a sense of humor, it has fangs, literally. Morrissey recounts watching her, in a pub, call over an elderly Englishman's meekly quivering terrier. "Do you know what dogs love?" she said to Morrissey. "They love THIS." Then the notorious animal rights activist picked up the pooch, put it on her lap, and sunk her teeth right into its neck. "The little dog clicks into a freeze-spasm like a kitten in its mother's mouth. The dog's owner and the dying bar staff watch stricken with horror."

Her bark and bite have sometimes bitten back at her. With Farndon and Wild, she now had a bassist and a drummer, but she got into a telephone altercation with Tony Secunda. It had to do with her offhandedly rehearsing and playing a gig with some friends who'd asked a favor—these were the Moors Murderers. The tabloids spread the word about a new band fronted by "Chrissie Hynd of the *NME*." The Moors Murderers were not amused; neither was Secunda, and neither was she. They argued, and he hung up on her. Her response was to decide never to speak to him again.

That left her without a manager, but she knew another bloke called Greg Shaw. She had once stayed up all night teaching him the chords to "Louie, Louie" (all three of them), which in turn taught her that she was a more accomplished guitarist than she realized, relative to most. Shaw was so grateful for the lesson that now, as the owner of a small record label, he wrote her a letter and told her he knew a young A&R (artists and repertoire) guy named Dave Hill, and that if she ever wanted to seek out a record deal he would put her in touch with him. She took the offer. Hill heard her play a little and stepped into Secunda's role, paying off her debts and giving her funds to keep her solvent so she could play music.

Kent, Verh, Wild, Shaw, Hill, Lemmy, Memmi, Secunda—no artist finds her way without angels like these. Some stayed longer than others. Some have long since disappeared; others she chased away. A few were Hell's Angels. But each of them found her and helped her move forward.

The effort to find another drummer to replace Wild instead netted her a guitar player—*the* guitar player. She hadn't actually given up on the idea of getting Phil Taylor, Lemmy's drummer from Motörhead, because she'd heard Motörhead were going to break up (which was why the Heartbreakers were said to be in on the bidding for him). But she didn't think it was all right to go straight at Taylor. As a ruse to get him to play with her, she told him she was planning to audition a guitarist and needed a drummer to sit in at the tryout. So now they needed a dupe guitarist. Pete Farndon knew a guy from back in Hereford named Jimmy; for a while, Jimmy had been in a band led by Mott the Hoople's ex-keyboardist and then he had played in a sort of Bad Company–lite combo.

What was Jimmy up to now?, Pete wondered. Working in a record shop back in Hereford, it turned out, growing veggies in his garden and being a dad to his little kid. Jimmy wasn't much interested in going back to London, but perhaps someone promised him drugs. Jimmy liked drugs, especially fast ones like speed and cocaine—not Chrissie Hynde's bag at all—but she consented in order get Taylor behind the drums. The songs she was writing at the time weren't really Jimmy's bag, either. He wasn't interested in punk at all: "too bloody loud."[32] He liked melodies and the Beatles; his favorite band was the Beach Boys. He was not a guitar showman, and he considered himself a rhythm guitarist, not lead. Later, when the Pretenders played live, that's how she introduced him: "On rhythm guitar, Jimmy Scott!"

James Honeyman-Scott is nearly as responsible for the Pretenders as Chrissie Hynde is. Meeting him was probably the single most important musical moment of her life. Without him, she doubts she'd have had any musical career to speak of. "I would have a basic song that wouldn't turn anybody's head, and Jimmy would start playing to it, and that's when it became a Pretenders song." He created what she called, with doctrinaire emphasis, "the Pretenders Guitar Sound," which was assiduously reproduced (to the degree that it could be) on the band's records after his death. The Pretenders Guitar Sound probably was not quite what she meant by Motorcycles with Guitars, but Scott filled her unfinished idea with the sound she hadn't known she'd been searching for all along.

Most important, Jimmy reawakened the melodist in her, the woman who had been kissed by Jackie Wilson and had grown up with the British Invasion and blues-rock and soul and R&B. The tuneful, sweet songs she'd soon be writing, like "Kid" and "Back on the Chain Gang," were unthinkable without him, even though he was already dead by the time the latter was recorded. But Jimmy never cared about songwriting credit even while he lived. Just five of the twenty-six Pretenders songs recorded before his death have his name on them, and he fiercely protected her exclusive ownership of the rest. After she succumbed to Farndon's demand for co-writing credit on "The Wait"—even though all he had done was suggest a key change on the bridge—Scott chastised her: "Don't *ever* give your songs away!" Evidence that she heeded his advice: Tony Butler, whose bass line catalyzed "My City Was Gone," did not receive co-writing credit for the song; nor did anyone else on *Learning to Crawl*, the first album she made after Scott died.

As soon as she started Jimmy's sham audition, she knew she was actually holding a real audition—and that he had landed the part of her guitarist. Taylor went back to Motörhead, but "I had to have Jimmy in the band," she decided, and she persuaded him to hang around and make a demo tape that included a cover of an obscure Kinks tune called "Stop Your Sobbing." Jimmy returned to Hereford, but she began plotting to lure him back.

Jimmy's main interest in the London music scene at the time had to do with pop maestro Nick Lowe and his associates: guys like Dave Edmunds and Billy Bremner from Lowe's band Rockpile.

If Lowe could be convinced to produce their band, Jimmy might be convinced to join it. She knew Lowe—she knew *everybody*, which was her primary currency in London—so she gave him the tape. Lowe listened to it and said he was interested in producing "this Sandie Shaw song"—he didn't realize "Stop Your Sobbing" was by the Kinks. "I was quivering with excitement when I called Jimmy Scott," she remembers, "'cause I knew all I had to say was Nick Lowe wants to produce a single with us and Jimmy would want to join the band."[33] But that turned out to be unnecessary. When she phoned Jimmy, before she could say anything—about Nick Lowe or anything else—he said he wanted in.

So they cut "Stop Your Sobbing" with Lowe, and Jimmy became a member of her combo—which now needed a name.

"Dave Hill called and said, 'Look, they're pressing this record now. What about a name?'" The night before Hill called her, she had been talking with a friend about a surreptitiously tenderhearted Hell's Angel she knew who would play Sam Cooke's version of the Platters' "The Great Pretender" when he was out of earshot of his fellow bikers. She was still thinking about that when her manager asked her to name her band. And that is how her enduring love, the Biker, christened her band as it released its first song, written by her most famous love, Ray Davies.

The only remaining issue was the drummer. The one who had replaced Wild wasn't good enough. Jimmy and Pete knew yet another Hereford guy. Jimmy had even been in a band with him. What had become of him? It turned out that Martin Chambers was living just a couple of blocks away from where they were staying in London. He was supporting himself as a driving instructor because he got a free car out of it. He had no band at the time and wanted to be in one. They were seeking a more muscular playing style than the one their drummer of the moment could manage, and Chambers had that style: he'd pound his kit nearly out of shape on tour. They invited him to sit in with them one night in rehearsal. "As soon as I heard Martin thumping away on 'Precious,'" she remembered,

"I started laughing so hard I had to turn my face to the wall. When I recovered my composure I turned to face the band I'd been searching for."

Jimmy Scott may have been the Pretender most responsible for creating the band's sound, but Martin Chambers was the one most responsible for legitimizing their continuity. Without him, it would have been harder for Chrissie Hynde to keep insisting on the Pretenders as a true band after Jimmy and Pete perished in the early eighties. And Chambers, though never the most technical of drummers, was always an excellent live player—boisterous, loud, joyful—and live performance was always an essential part of her picture of rock music since she had cut her teeth on going to shows. Yet touring was not easy for her to undertake, given her band's limited output and her long layoffs to raise children. She needed someone who didn't require seasoning and, more important, who had helped build the Pretenders and had its DNA in him—someone whose very presence on stage could verify, for her and her fans, that these really were the Pretenders, not just Chrissie Hynde and some hired guns going by that name. Steadfast and loyal despite occasional and sometimes lengthy layoffs, Chambers has been in and out of the band throughout its existence, nearly thirty years. His relationship with his paymaster has not always been cordial—no surprise, given his multiple dismissals—but who would have guessed that the last soldier mustered in, the third drummer she tried, would be the only other original Pretender to survive and endure?

It was all in place, then, but there was a problem. Nick Lowe wasn't interested in producing their full album. He had only liked their version of "Stop Your Sobbing," not her songs. She would get her revenge on *Pretenders II*, in a song called "Pack It Up": "I see your dog got shot. Well, hell, never mind. That's show biz, big boy. You've got to be cruel to be kind." For now, though, she had business to attend to, and Dave Hill landed another producer of note, Chris Thomas, who had gotten his start as a youngster under

George Martin on the Beatles' *White Album* and had later worked with Pink Floyd, Roxy Music, and many others. Thomas also produced the Sex Pistols' *Never Mind the Bollocks*, which sounds a good deal more polished and sophisticated than punk is supposed to: "a normal pro rock record with Johnny Rotten singing," as one veteran producer put it.[34]

Thomas's fluency in both punk and pop was a perfect match for the Pretenders' split sensibility: a pop heart beating at punk volume; punk attitude with pop chops. Hill got them signed, without much ceremony, to Sire Records, and they went into the studio together in 1979 and made their first album, which was full of singles to mine for the radio. Three of them hit the charts before *Pretenders* even came out: "Stop Your Sobbing," "Kid," and "Brass in Pocket," which shot to number one a month before the LP's release and made the Pretenders a suddenly hot commodity. Hill was so sure of the band that after the deal with Sire was signed, he quit his own dinky record label and devoted himself to managing them full-time. He was twenty-six, two years younger than three of the Pretenders. All they had to do was deliver an album that would hold its singles together. Did they ever.

TWO

UP THE NECK

Pretenders

*My philosophy and where I'm coming from and why I do this
has always been exactly the same. And it's all ultimately about
child protection and what you might call animal rights. That's
something I've had with me since early on.*

—CHRISSIE HYNDE, INTERVIEW ON BLUERAILROAD.COM, 2010

Pretenders is one of rock's greatest debut albums. *Rolling Stone* has it thirteenth, right after *The Clash*, by Chrissie Hynde's London peers. *The Clash* was released just two years earlier, in 1977, part of a raft of landmark debuts made between 1976 and 1979: *Ramones*; *Never Mind the Bollocks, Here's the Sex Pistols*; *Talking Heads: 77*, Elvis Costello's *My Aim Is True*; Television's *Marquee Moon*; Wire's *Pink Flag*; and *Outlandos d'Amour*, by the Police.[1] *Boston* and *Van Halen* appeared too.[2] There was also the strange and strangely underrated *Q: Are We Not Men? A: We Are Devo!*, which paired Mark Mothersbaugh and Brian Eno, an unexpected joining of players from Chrissie Hynde's musical worlds past and near-present, American and English. There was stiff competition for new bands to get noticed in the late seventies, on both sides of the Atlantic. New York was in thrall to its CBGB revolution. Punk and its post-punk heirs were on fire in London. New music had to be not only good but audacious. Perhaps the higher achievement of *Pretenders* is not that it's one of the best debuts of all time but that it's one of the best debuts of its own time.

One of *Pretenders'* greatest audacities is its running time: forty-seven minutes. This was a band of seasoned players with a lot of music already in them, and they weren't holding any of it back. They didn't pad songs with long solos or extraneous choruses or fadeouts. This is legitimate, purposeful music from a band already fluent in a wide range of styles. *Pretenders* incorporates punk, reggae, soul, rock, power pop, rockabilly, and even a sort of "easy-listening," as the pop musician Scott Miller later described the band's softer side.[3] Yet the influences have been fully absorbed; every song sounds unmistakably like the Pretenders, thanks to Jimmy Scott's distinctive guitar and of course to the Great Pretender's idiosyncratic, inimitable voice, which producer Chris Thomas smartly pushed way up in the mix, with the strong rhythm section of Farndon and Chambers providing depth and propulsion underneath. This is more than a "promising debut." *Pretenders* fulfills the band's promise completely. Many listeners think they never matched it again.

Another of the debut's audacities is its almost audible leap from punk into music that is anything but. *Pretenders* leads off with a pair of bruising, punk-rooted songs, as though confirming the prevailing musical standard, but the album quickly expands its reach (and vastly improves on punk's generally amateurish musicianship). By side two, the Pretenders have left punk almost entirely behind them. If Kinks covers, unabashed reggae and soul influences, and a staunchly woman-led rock group seemed to run counter to their London moment, they were actually quite timely in terms of the one to follow. With the Sex Pistols–led surge already receding by 1979, *Pretenders* was one of the major forces towing London music into new waters—not least because the album was a hit on both sides of the Atlantic. *Postpunk* can be a vague term, but certainly *Pretenders* is a significant postpunk feat: it offers a new, previously unimaginable direction for popular music after punk.

Perhaps the most significant thing about *Pretenders* is its bold, complex, articulate expression of the ideas and feelings that will consume Chrissie Hynde for the rest of her career. Listening to *Pretenders* in hindsight reveals not only a fully realized album but also the blueprint for all the albums that follow. It is at once the precocious firstborn child and the DNA for all the others.

The first song on *Pretenders*, "Precious," is one of the more pugnacious album openers from an era of pugnacious rock: it actually does sound a lot like Motorcycles with Guitars, as do three of the album's first four songs. Chris Thomas was no stranger to this sort of thing. He was, after all, the man at the controls for *Never Mind the Bollocks, Here's the Sex Pistols* just two years earlier. That album's lead track, "Holidays in the Sun," comes marching out of the speakers (almost literally: it opens with the sound of stomping boots) with a descending run of guitar chords that lands hard on the tonic floor and keeps going up and then coming down, relentlessly. "Precious" is in some ways a similar song. The crunchy guitar sound would fit just fine on *Never Mind the Bollocks*. An insistent opening verse that is slightly less rancorous than Johnny Rotten's Belsen-bound nihilism concludes with "shitting bricks" because the singer is so wound up that she can't stand it anymore. (And this is only the album's first song!) The guitar then takes a phase-shifting rocket booster into the chorus, playing a descending line of chords that recalls "Holidays in the Sun": "Made me wanna, made me wanna, you made me make it!" The vocal climax is tagged with the coming-down afterthought, "Oh, you're so mean."

A ruthless one-night stand ensues. The guy bruises her hip while putting it to her in the Sterling Hotel: "a hooker hotel," as one description put it, and a general "haven for criminal activities" during the seventies. (In *Reckless*, she somehow recalls a mescaline-fueled sexcapade in one of its rooms.) Afterward, they drive around Cleveland in an old Imperial with nothing much to do; she'll be driving around with nothing much to do in "Brass in Pocket," later on the album. "Round and round and round and round the Shoreway"—a traffic-clogged emblem of Cleveland's car culture—they're a "duet, duet, duet, duet on the pavement." The sly wordplay on "do it" is reinforced in the next line: she worries (or perhaps fantasizes) about getting pregnant. And then: "Oh, we duet all night."

She's tempted to hang around longer in dead-end Cleveland, but notes that its local-color characters (Howard the Duck, a Cleveland creation; and Mr. Stress, a beloved bluesman) are "trapped in a world that they never made": the world of car culture. So she blows off the whole scene: "Not me baby, I'm too precious. I had to fuck off"—to London, one imagines, never to return. We've become inured to profanity in music, but it was almost unheard-of in popular music at the time, especially in censorious England. (In 2014, *New Yorker* music critic Sasha Frere-Jones wrote, "Hynde was the first person I heard singing the word 'fuck.'")[4] Ending a song with "I had to fuck off" was a serious provocation, along with Jimmy Scott's guitar solo: a repetitive two-note wail that exactly mimics the sound of a police siren zooming in and out in pursuit of the Imperial, which she's "got my eye on," as if she's considering stealing it. Not long after that, the song hammers its way to a no-nonsense ending.

Rock critic Kurt Loder noted the Pretenders' "treacherously erratic meter" in a 1980 *Rolling Stone* profile,[5] and we first hear it on the album's second song, "The Phone Call." The unusual time signature implies a skipped beat, like an arrhythmic heart or a mind on speed; uncontrolled urgency; and a loss of bearings, which the sound and lyrics of "The Phone Call" reinforce. It's technically not even a song: there's no singing. After some telephone sound effects (recorded from an actual phone by John Cale, of all people), we hear a spoken-word voicemail message from "a faceless messenger who doesn't want to see you hit." The caller warns the listener that a "winged demon" is back in town and in pursuit, although it's difficult to make out the words. The vocal is double-tracked, but the two tracks sound staggered and blurry, and occasionally a third iteration of her voice further scrambles intelligibility. The overall effect is of menace, uncertainty, and paranoia. Someone or something is out to get you, whoever you are.

When "The Phone Call" gives in to the almost inevitable concession of 4/4 time, it swaps out its "treacherously erratic meter" for an equally treacherous key change: the whole song plummets by a vertiginous tritone, which used to be considered "the Devil's Interval." (Liszt used it to connote Hell in the "Dante Sonata.") This change of key is apparently the bridge—although it's hard to discern the song's structure.

Not just her meter but Chrissie Hynde's entire compositional strategy was treacherously erratic early on; we're hearing the oddly conceived patents of an inventor who hasn't entirely grasped her medium. Years later she recalled that in her younger, naïve beginnings as a composer, some of her songs so completely violated form that they didn't even have choruses. But violation of form creates new forms, and that is part of *Pretenders'* audacity. "I feel inventive," she sings later on the album, on the definitive "Brass in Pocket." She's talking about prowling the nightlife and attracting "attention—give it to me," but she might just as easily be describing the disconcerting originality in her early songwriting. Although "The Phone Call" hangs around in 4/4 time for a stretch, it also throws in a measure of 3/4 here, another of 6/4 there. It leaps back to its original key and then right back off of it again. A synthesizer joins the fray, like interference from another phone line, and just as the song is about to go totally haywire, it finally crashes back into its original key and its 7/4 meter, and breathlessly concludes its message—as though the speaker was busy making arrangements during the frenetic instrumental break: a ticket out of town has now been bought for the listener, who nonetheless must "accept no parcels in the mail." We'll never know what those parcels might contain, because the song abruptly ends in a beeping dial tone—it goes literally off the hook.

We go from off the hook to up the neck, but first it might be worth assessing where *Pretenders* has gone in its first two songs.

The answer is simple: Danger! The songs' characters are in situations they must escape; if they don't, bad things will happen to them. Bad things already have happened, in fact, and will again, none of them worse than those on the brutal "Tattooed Love Boys," two songs away. This is the psychological legacy of the Heavy Bikers, a rendering of all the harrowing experiences Chrissie Hynde suffered in the early and mid-seventies. As she told Kurt Loder in 1980:

> "I had a terrible time. I was hitchhiking around, and I'd forgotten how dangerous it was. I had a few bad experiences, but the way I look at it now is, for every sort of act of sodomy I was forced to perform, I'm getting paid ten thousand pounds now." She laughs bitterly. "That's how I try to look at it, anyway."[6]

"Any experience is better than no experience," she thought in her youth. But the consequences of bad experience can be severe, and repeated blows triggered a strong protective mechanism—protection of others even more than of herself. She takes abuse in "Precious" and tries to save someone else from it in "The Phone Call." Her trademark makeup of heavy kohl can be read as a pair of black eyes. "I'm a mother!" she bellows fifteen years later, in the title of a song on *Last of the Independents*. She has had the maternal instinct "with me since early on," and not just toward children and animals. Her songs also mourn and protest destruction of the natural environment, which she saw befalling her Ohio home even as a child. The setting of "Precious" is heavy with concrete-jungle imagery and sound, especially traffic: pavement, an old car, a police siren, and Cleveland's busy Shoreway. The relationship between the environment and animals is obvious enough, but she perceptively widens it to it include children: that most vulnerable part of our ecology.

"Precious" and "The Phone Call," arresting as they are, scarcely hint that the Pretenders have their next song in them, but they launch into "Up the Neck" almost before "The Phone Call" has even ended, jumping right in after its pulsing busy signal with a similarly pulsing guitar riff at exactly the same tempo, as if "Up the Neck" is meant to continue the disconnected thought of the previous song. The rest of the band joins in to pin this riff down in the key of F-major, but the ensuing vamp jumps to A-major—an unpredictable modulation that somehow sounds perfectly normal (the song will return to F-major soon enough). From here, the intro unfolds into a straightforward 4/4 meter and two-chord progression, framed by a pair of Scott's simple, three-note guitar licks—which both go up the neck.

In 1977, when his debut album came out, Elvis Costello told *NME*, "The only two things that matter to me, the only motivation for me to write all these songs, are revenge and guilt. Those are the only emotions I know about." Chrissie Hynde, on the other hand, didn't need to tell an interviewer what her two guiding emotions were, because she announces them at the opening of "Up the Neck":

> *Anger and lust.*

There it is, clear and concise. And there, too, is her singing voice, just now making its first full appearance on *Pretenders*' third song. On "Precious" and "The Phone Call" she only spoke, hissed, spat, or shouted. Now she croons:

> *My senses running amok,*
> *Bewildered and deluded.*
> *Have I been hit by a truck?*

From truculent to "hit by a truck" (and more traffic imagery): the collision releases her instantly identifiable alto, tremulous and full and expressive. It will be with us for the next three and a half decades, virtually unchanged from its 1978 beginnings to 2014, but it will have revealed much of its extraordinary emotional range by the time "Up the Neck" ends. Chrissie Hynde's voice—more than her songwriting, her trailblazing as a "woman in rock," her iconic and unmistakable look and attitude—is why she's a legend. It isn't a tutored voice, nor could it have been. "Distinctive voices in rock," she writes in *Reckless*, "are trained through years of many things: frustration, fear, loneliness, anger, insecurity, arrogance, narcissism, or just sheer perseverance. Anything but a teacher."

Yet all singers are trained by the voices they love best. In her case, that's the voice of Tim Buckley, her "favorite singer of all time." Her voice resembles Buckley's in some ways, including her tendency toward affectation—but it's her *natural* affectation, not a deliberate style. She could no more change it than Robert Plant could change his. And like Plant's, her voice's function is not only to deliver language; sometimes she uses it as an instrument, a lead guitar of sorts, sounding and shaping notes.

Throughout her career, she has often sung lines that are only partially intelligible. We can look up her lyrics now and sing along—"Brass in Pocket" is the cardinal example of a lyric set that has to be consulted on paper before it can be sung—but in the moment of hearing her, we feel what she sings without needing to comprehend its literal meaning. The way she enunciates—or rather, doesn't quite enunciate—the word "truck" in the first verse of "Up the Neck," eliding the "r" so the word sounds like "tuck," as though she's slurring, precisely conveys the feeling of being knocked flat by drugs or sex or pain or all three. When at the end of each verse she drops into a lower register, choked and unsteady, it's with "a headache that split my skull, alone in a room." We're literally up the neck: that is, in her pounding head, the true setting of all the drama of this song told in flashback. And its title is an invitation to stop prioritizing her body, which has never been her calling card: stop trying to get in her pants; get in her mind instead.

"Up the Neck" seems to take much of its material from an episode in *Reckless*: a one-night stand in the Hotel Sterling gone very wrong, as you might expect of anything that begins with hitchhiking. The verse opens on the morning after, with a sunny A-major riff that doesn't hint at the bleakness to come. She's thinking about the night before, "when my tongue lay inside of his lip" and it "felt like the time in the womb" (sex, but also mothering and child protection, obliquely). Then the song drops back to down to F-major, the key where it began, and thuds like a headache as she sing-speaks her way toward the resolution:

> *I got down on the floor with my head pressed between my knees*
> *Under the bed with my teeth sunk into my own flesh*

We return to A-major as she sings the payoff line, the only line that will repeat in the song:

> *I said, "Baby, ah, sweetheart."*

This is not exactly a chorus, and the title phrase is never sung, but the chorus is actually right there, slyly, under "Baby, ah, sweetheart": the guitar runs four chords, A-B-C-D, right up the neck.

The next verse continues the flashback, a sex scene told in painful, short-story detail—Alice Munro could have written it. They're going at it on the rug, but her eyes aren't closed in passion—far from it. Underneath her, "something was sticking to the shag rug" (with bonus wordplay on "shag"), and then she notices the tile floor where the rug ends, an echo from *Reckless* of "the black-and-white floor tile shrinking and expanding in the foyer of the Hotel Sterling," her senses running amok on mescaline. But in her mind, she isn't on that rug at all; she's already in the next morning, or even further into the future. "I remember the way he groaned, and moved with an animal skill." The skill, of course, is not in giving her any pleasure; it's in bringing himself to orgasm, while she "rubbed [her] face in the sweat that ran down his chest" and observed with unaroused detachment that "it was all very run of the mill."

There is no eros in this act of coitus, and her matter-of-fact, fragmentary, slightly arrhythmic delivery of lines that don't scan well contribute to the lack of feeling: you have to read them on the page in order to notice that they rhyme ("slug"/"rug"; "skill"/"mill"), and she has to cram some of the syllables into their measures. This awkward but nonetheless apposite phrasing may partly owe to the song's tempo, which is faster in the final version than in its original composition. Jimmy Scott recalled that "Up the Neck" had originally been composed as something more like a reggae song. "Let's speed it up,"[7] he suggested, which forced her to squeeze the lines into a shorter metrical space. She has long made a habit of this peculiar stratagem, which summons a different part of her voice—the part that is reactive, inventive.

The Pretenders' reggae influence is much stronger than is regularly acknowledged, and it's essential for understanding their music. There are apparitions of reggae on nearly all of the band's releases (they're especially prominent on 2002's *Loose Screw*), a reminder that this genre, like punk, was also burgeoning in London in the seventies. It's quite evident in the early music of the Clash and Elvis Costello. In its own way, reggae was more punk than punk: farther outside mainstream musical culture, and racially marginalized—music of the oppressed. She wrote some of the songs on *Pretenders* while she was living in Ladbroke Grove, a neighborhood heavily populated by Rastafarians. Along with the other "teachers" of her voice—"frustration, fear, loneliness," Tim Buckley—reggae must be included.

As the narrator's lover reaches orgasm, "I noticed his scent started to change somehow." It's that "animal skill" again, detectable in the beast's very smell. We are brought uncomfortably close, right into the space between their chests. We feel his sweat, smell his scent, and then "his face went berserk and the veins bulged on his brow." As he comes, the narrator can only repeat what she has said in the first verse. "I said, 'Baby, ah, sweetheart.'" But now we don't know if she says it to him or herself.

It's hard to think of a franker, more joyless and disturbing sex scene in American popular song. In a genre of music that celebrates sex, is literally named for it, here is one of its most passionless examples. This sex is all bestial exertion and secretion, not love or even lust, which has been converted into its equal and opposite: "Lust turns to anger," she sang at the beginning of the verse. Lust and anger are part of the same volatile substance, but only anger is present here on the shag rug.

After a repetitive, choked, almost Robert Fripp–like guitar solo by Scott, lust gets further complicated in the third verse's perplexing first line: "Bondage to lust, abuse of facility." "Blackmailed emotions" follow—they'll follow her throughout the album, especially in "Private Life"—but they're no longer hers alone: these emotions "confuse the demon and devotee" alike. (Is this the same "winged demon"—and, for that matter, insinuations of blackmail—that menaced "The Phone Call"?) She is convinced that both of them had "sweet intentions," but then she gets off one of her characteristically bitter and trenchant lines: "A wish is a shot in the dark when your coin's down the well." So much for intentions.

The coda brings the danger back into the picture—just a hint of it, a sense of shadowing menace as "I got myself out in the hall with my teeth in my head up to my neck," as though lucky not to have had them knocked out, and as though she already has the headache coming on: that awful pounding feeling in the teeth. And then the song touches bottom: "I said . . . said . . . said: *dead*." She delivers the word "dead" flatly and tonelessly, like a death blow, her voice joined by a duplicate of itself, as though echoing in the corridor of the Sterling. (After the parallel version of the incident in *Reckless*, the guy she was with told her that the only woman he'd ever been in love with was "dead. Dead. *Dead*." Then he threatened to kill her.) And then, again: "Baby, ah, sweetheart," for the third time, and this time it sounds like a deep, sighing lament for anyone who needs it.

The band sits there waiting, vamping, almost panting on that unresolved F-major. Then she lets loose with a long, loud, plaintive, "Ohhhhhhhhhh!" It's as far up the neck as she has gone. We'll hear this *Ohhhhhhhhhh!* from her again and again over the years: her trademark quavering wail, almost a sob, which has in it the desperation of a primal scream and a cry for help, or even salvation. This is the song's true climax.

Yet, even after *dead*, and its subsequent *Ohhhhhhhhhh!*, "Up the Neck" is still not done. As the narrator stands there *Ohhhhhhh*ing in the hallway, the song goes "apewire"—a word she coins out of "haywire" and "apeshit" in *Pretenders'* next track. From the familiar F-major riff, a source of intermediary comfort in this most uncomfortable of songs, the song completely loses its screws—willfully unscrews them, actually. First Farndon's bass jumps up a major third, as if trying to return from F back to the tonal center of A-major, where the tune's verses lived. But the rest of the band does not follow. The bass obediently returns to F, Chambers moves to the ride cymbal—a solid, tried-and-true fadeout move—but then, during the fade, the bass loses its grip altogether on F, or any key for that matter, and the guitars sound like their strings and springs are popping out as they spiral out of control (up the neck, of course), in the song's last few audible bars. It's as though the narrator, "bewildered and deluded" just as she said, is running for cover in a hail of violent derangement.

The next song is "Tattooed Love Boys," set to another jittery 7/4 meter, but the time signature alternates with 4/4, making the song even harder to count off than if it stuck to 7/4. Scott plays an "Up the Neck"–like guitar figure, but faster and higher, as though it's still got a screw loose from the end of the previous song, like a jack-in-the-box with its springs sprung. That sets the stage for her account of her assault by the Heavy Bikers in Cleveland, as *Reckless* makes clear. It was a brutal encounter. "I shot my mouth off and you showed me what that hole was for," she spits. The tattooed love boys spit back: "Stop sniveling, you're gonna make some plastic surgeon a rich man!" She'll be nothing but "another human interest story," a hapless crime victim reduced to a column-inch or two deep in the Metro section: "You—are—that," she pronounces, leaving spaces between the words that are surely filled by blows. Then the song ends as abruptly as a door (or a fist) slamming in her face.

The instrumental "Space Invader," a straight-driving, power-chord, heavy-rock number, provides a break from this opening quartet of harrowing songs. Perhaps it's intended as a personal soundtrack to the video game. (Sound effects sampled from the game are audible as the track ends.) One of the first video games on the mass market, Space Invaders was a sensation in the late seventies, and the phrase itself had been in the musical air since the moon landing. David Bowie included a line about it on *Ziggy Stardust* before the game even existed, with his classic prescience, and Rush makes a reference on the prog-rock juggernaut "Tom Sawyer." Invented in 1978, Space Invaders quickly swept the globe, and it's easy to imagine band members killing a fair number of hours playing it during the Pretenders' downtime.

After "Space Invader" comes "The Wait," a song Chrissie Hynde wrote about Farndon's youth spent hanging about in arcades. Like "Up the Neck," it was originally slower than its final form. In the upbeat, rockabilly-influenced number, she rat-a-tats barely intelligible lines, racing to keep up with the accelerated meter, which is complicated by a more erratic measure: a bar of 2/4 thrown in after the standard 4/4s of each line:

> *The wait child pinball child pool hall child hurts*
> *The wait child pacing child forth back now hurts*
> *The wait child neon light late night lights hurt*

The word *hurt* or *hurts* ends every line of the three verses, which suggest a portrait of an abused boy not just in the arcade but also out in the street, perhaps a runaway: bus stops, platform walks;

"bruised," "slapped," "felled." It's "gonna hurt some," she promises (or warns) the kid. The song draws on one of the bases of the two-part philosophy she'd had with her "since early on": child protection. In this case, though, there's nothing she can do for the poor kid.

"Stop Your Sobbing"—that "Sandie Shaw song," as Nick Lowe heard it—closes side one, although it was the first song the band ever recorded. It was written by Ray Davies, of course, but it also evokes Lowe's own "Cruel to Be Kind," which had been a big transatlantic hit the previous year. And not just in its production: both songs' lyrics wrap kindness in cruelty; they are chipper while they chap. The sweetly lilting, country-tinged "Stop Your Sobbing" exudes Davies's hallmark cheer, but his cheer is deceptive (as it often is). He's not so much comforting as admonishing: if you want me back, you'd better dry your eyes now. Still, the song closes side one on an upbeat note, and Chrissie Hynde adds extra upbeats to Davies's more restrained original vocal: "Stop-stop-stop-stop stop your sobbing now-ohhh!" she sings as the final chorus fades out. It is the only song on side one to make that graceful exit other than "Up The Neck"—which falls apart in the fadeout.

Side two of *Pretenders* takes on a different hue from side one, leaving punk far, far behind. It's generally slower, mellower, and softer in sound and spirit: anger and lust are tinged with compassion, melancholy, and tenderness. It has fewer changes of meter and key. The opener, "Kid," is a companion piece to "Stop Your Sobbing,"—another "don't cry" tune—but its similar lightness of tone also conceals a darker story and message, and has another key change lurking on the bridge. The song, she explained, "is about a kid who finds out his mother's a prostitute"[8]: "I know you know what I'm about / I won't deny it / But you forgive though you don't understand." It's easy to imagine the kid as the young Pete Farndon in "The Wait," killing time in arcades and train stations while his mom works the streets. Again, the issue is child protection. "Precious kid," she calls the child, echoing *Pretenders*' first

47

song title, and the stance is typical for her: she's endangering herself for the sake of the child. The song ends with another *Ohhh-hhhhhhh*—this one drawn out, harmonized, melismatic; poignant rather than feral or desperate.

From the protective instinct comes a need for privacy, a theme that will recur throughout her songwriting career and is first made explicit on the next song, "Private Life." The slow reggae tune, which was a top-twenty UK hit for Grace Jones in 1980, slinks along, always circling back to the same line: "Your private life drama, baby, leave me out," the narrator sings over and over again, with the implicit reciprocal insistence that the listener stay out of hers. Later in the song, underneath this repeated line, the men in the band sing, in falsetto, "You've been lying to someone, and now me"—the "someone" presumably being the wife on whom the man has been cheating with the narrator of the song. Ingeniously the song finds a way to attack the philanderer with two voices at once. Now the narrator, his mistress, is discarding him. "You asked me for advice, I said use the door," she spits. It's one of the great kiss-off lines of Chrissie Hynde's career.

Then along comes "Brass in Pocket," the signature song in the Pretenders' catalog, a smash transatlantic hit, and probably the single for which the Pretenders will be remembered. But its composer doesn't much care for it: "It doesn't know what it wants to be."[9] She didn't want it released as a single and was embarrassed when it went to No. 1: "If I heard it in a Woolworth's, I would have to run out." To her, "Brass in Pocket" was a throwaway. "It's just me trying to write like 'The Boys Are Back in Town,'"[10] singing in the voice of Thin Lizzy's "chick that used to dance a lot. Every night she'd be on the floor shaking what she'd got."

It's probably the simplest song on *Pretenders*, built around a little guitar riff she heard Jimmy Scott noodling with one day. It has four chords—five, if you want to nitpick—and no bridge. The song thumps along in a confident but modest midtempo 4/4, and it doesn't provide a platform for one of Chrissie Hynde's better vocal performances. She sounds hemmed in and strained as she keeps pounding at the same high phrases, or sliding and slurring around words she doesn't know quite how to deliver. The song's dramatic tension comes entirely from the choice to sit almost tauntingly on an unresolved V chord as she sings, almost warns: "Gonna use my arms/ legs/ style/ sidestep/ fingers/ (my-my-my) 'magination."

Did you know it was "sidestep"? How much of "Brass in Pocket," the Pretenders' most famous song, long beloved and sung along with ("I'm special!" *"Special!"*), can you actually sing, verse for verse? Of its twenty-one discrete lines, six contain at least one word that is either disputed or hard to understand. It isn't just the difficulty of hearing "intention / I feel inventive" or the line that has "new skank" (dance moves) and "so reet" (righteous ones), but stranger argot that nearly requires an annotator. After you've settled on "Detroit leaning" in the second verse, message boards will explain that the narrator is not actually in Detroit. The "Detroit Lean" is a street-stylish way of driving a car: you put your right hand on the wheel at twelve o'clock while you lean way back in the seat and cock your head to the left.

"Brass in Pocket" has beguiled listeners for years, and perhaps its possible range of meaning accounts for its enduring popularity. What is "brass in pocket," after all? It's another slang term from England, where she heard a guy picking up his suit at the dry cleaner's ask, "Was there any brass in pocket?"—that is, had he left any money in the suit? The song's brass in pocket is a different kind of currency: confidence, attitude, brassiness. The word *swag*, with its twin connotations of lucre and self-assurance, perfectly captures the dual meaning. The second line's "Got bottle"—not "Bible" or "bile," as it's sometimes misheard—is another English slang term that means confidence.

The original meaning of "brass in pocket," money, later came to the song by other means. For anyone familiar with the video, it's almost impossible not to picture it when the song plays. The Pretenders were formed not long before MTV's debut, and they were perfect for the new medium. They had a distinctive-looking (and, importantly, white) female singer with a strong, charismatic presence, who naturally applied her mother's "striking flair for color and design"[11] to her makeup and dress, backed by three high-energy guys with stylish hair who could carry off some fashion and look good playing their instruments. "Brass in Pocket" was the seventh video ever played on MTV, one of five Pretenders videos to air on the new network's first broadcast day in 1981. Ironically, Chrissie Hynde deplores music videos. Their inauthenticity is intolerable to her, and she hates making them.

The other MTV video from the band's debut album was for "Kid"; the additional three were all from *Pretenders II*, which was already out by the time of MTV's debut. An older song like "Brass in Pocket" was retroactively claimed, along with many other slightly outdated singles that appeared as videos in the summer of 1981. The video for "Brass in Pocket" remained in heavy rotation during MTV's first months, and some part of the song's international popularity must have owed to its frequent appearance on this secondary singles market.

The video for "Brass in Pocket" is simple and quite dopey, like many early videos. Chrissie Hynde plays a waitress, that occupation from which music saved her, in a mostly empty diner. There's almost literally "nobody else here," and certainly "no one like me." The only other body in the joint is a drunk slumped over his table. She tries to roust him right after pocketing some brass—a tip of a few coins. The other three Pretenders pull up in a shiny, attention-getting vintage car with tailfins (evoking the Imperial from "Precious"). They take a table, and she sings some of the song's lyrics at them. When she gets to "I'm special," Jimmy Scott shows the camera the menu with its "SPECIAL" paper-clipped to the front (the video's lone stab at cleverness). Meanwhile, she and Farndon, the two dark-haired Pretenders—and a real-life couple at the time—are starting to generate some heat, exchanging come-on looks, but then the guys' three girlfriends bounce into the diner and join them. Farndon's girl pokes him angrily when she catches him making eyes at the waitress, and it's only a few more seconds until all six exit the joint without having ordered, leaving Chrissie Hynde gazing longingly out the window as she sings the song's final chorus.

Ironically, the video shows her meeting the trio of musicians who got her out of her diner job for good. That they then leave her there is another irony, given that two of her three bandmates died within two years, and she would have to reinvent the Pretenders or (in the worst-case scenario) go back to tip wages. But the success of "Brass in Pocket" ensured that she'd never be a waitress again.

"Lovers of Today" follows "Brass in Pocket." It's a composition in two very distinct parts, awkwardly conjoined. The first part is that most musical expression of tending to children, a lullaby, one of several she'd compose over the years. "Please don't cry," she coos. "Hush, hush, hush, hush, baby sleep tight now." She warns that "all of the leaves come down every time babies cry": again, there's that link between protecting children and environmental damage. Later in the song, when babies dream, the birds sing. But just as we've settled in for a sweet melodic song, "Lovers of Today" pivots on an ominous chord and changes to a minor key, motivated by a radical change in the narrative: "Nobody wants to see lovers of today happy, so assume they're going to part," she sings, mournfully. Everyone's afraid of being "left with a broken heart." The song is suddenly no longer about children but about lovers—a different kind of baby—but before it develops its new subject, it quickly reverts to its initial major-key lullaby. Yet it can't stay there; something has been irremediably torn. It again gives way to the darker, minor-key lament about doomed romance. This time, however, it dispenses with lyrics altogether, using the minor-key signifier alone to create mood and latent drama, even melodrama, as the chords and drums get heavier and heavier, while Scott breaks off a searing guitar solo—not a characteristic one for him. There is another return to the lullaby, but once again the song veers down into lugubriousness, with the vocals weightily double-tracked before she concludes, in the fadeout, with a defiant one-liner that functions as a manifesto: "I'll never feel like a man in a man's world."

"Lovers of Today" would make an awkward, confused album closer, a lullaby gone wrong, but *Pretenders* has one more song to sing. "Mystery Achievement" boasts one of the Pretenders' catchiest choruses, and it's a testament to the sheer consistency of the quality of their debut that a song this infectious could be buried at the end of the album, almost an afterthought. "Mystery Achievement" opens as a driving soul number in C-minor, a two-chord vamp—first drums, then bass, then guitars, joining in one by one in old-fashioned style. The subject is fool's gold, false promises, empty success: the achievements are less mysterious than dubious. It's obvious what they are: gold records, sold-out shows, fancy clothes. Chrissie Hynde accuses these achievements of breathing down her neck (we've gone from up the neck to down it), declaring that if anyone gives her trophies, she'll only "sign them away." This is her brief but important first renunciation of worldly things, absorbed from the *Bhagavad Gita*, which she'll reaffirm more explicitly later in her career. All she wants to do is get out on the floor and dance the Cuban Slide. Soon she'll borrow that step for the title of a wonderful song on the subsequent *Extended Play*.

But there's always that tug, that longing to be a rock star: to be famous, popular, successful. When "Mystery Achievement" reaches the chorus, the song leaps up to a major key—a musical attitude adjustment—and she sings, "But every day, every night-time I find: mystery achievement, you're on my mind," even though the chorus ends with her renouncing that achievement again—it's "so unreeeeal," she sings as the song returns to its minor key. The mirage of hitting the big time, the desire to live the dream despite knowing it's nothing more than a dream—part of the mystery of the achievement is trying to figure out why you're pursuing it in the first place. Chrissie Hynde never wanted to be famous or thought she should be. But she was wise enough to know that she had to agree to play the character of rock star and accept some of the admittedly seductive and satisfying material trappings that came with the role of bandleader.

In the second verse, she carps, "Where's my sandy beach? I had my dreams like everybody else but they're out of reach." It's too late for her, and anyway "your demands are unending," she complains to the mystery achievement, which of course she hasn't achieved yet. Maybe it was never worth the trouble to begin with. "I've got no tears on my ice cream," she boasts, "but you know me: I love pretending."

That last line, which embeds her band's name, is a masterstroke. She makes it clear that she understands not only that the rock and roll fantasy is just that, a fantasy, but also that its unreality is precisely what makes it so desirable. All of this is makebelieve, dress-up, an escape from the diner: an alternate world of fame and fans and finery and music videos and the cover of *Rolling Stone*: all ice cream, no tears. The shape of the mystery achievement is not going to be revealed because it has no shape: the achievement is the mystery itself; pretending is the real thing; thus the Pretenders.

Reality—in the form of the mystery achievement itself—was lurking just around the corner.

THREE

BIRDS OF PARADISE

Extended Play and *Pretenders II*

> *Look round the room*
> *Life is unkind*
> *We fall but we keep getting up*
> *Over and over and over and over and over and over and over*
> *and over and over and over*

—"MESSAGE OF LOVE"

Songwriting, Chrissie Hynde said late in her career, is "like working on a jigsaw puzzle. It doesn't make any sense until you find that last piece."[1] Sometimes, though, you find the last piece first and construct the puzzle around it.

Playing the *Songwriters Circle* show in 1999, she explained the origins of "Talk of the Town." She strummed a B7 chord on her guitar and said, "I discovered this chord about twenty years ago, and I showed it to James Honeyman-Scott. He called it 'a Beatles chord,' and I wrote the song around that."[2] (She hasn't revealed whether the title has anything to do with the contemporaneous London club of the same name, now known again by its original name, the Hippodrome. The Pretenders don't seem to have ever played there, but a picture of the band in front of the venue appears in *Reckless*; clearly she knew the place, and she may simply have been taking some apt poetic license with the name.) Leaving aside that "Talk of the Town" uses the B7 chord only three times, as nothing more than a diving board into its verses, there's nothing inherently "Beatles chord" about B7, nor any particular

54

obscurity that should require that it be "discovered." She simply wasn't quite sure what to do with it until Scott gave her a musical setting on which to mount it: mid-period Beatles.

She already had the lyrical setting. "I had in mind this kid who used to stand outside the sound checks on our first tour, and I never spoke to him.[3] I remember the last time I saw him, I just left him standing in the snow. I never had anything to say to him. And I kind of wrote ['Talk of the Town'] for him."[4] Out of apparent regret over ignoring him, she wrote a warm and tender song about longing (the sheer act of writing a song for him is warm and tender too). That longing is why not only the leading B7 but the entire chord structure of "Talk of the Town" is apt. The song begins on G-major, the tonic chord. The intro canters along, with the guitars vamping between G and C while the bass sticks to G as an anchor. Some horsey momentum is provided by a sliding grace note of F-sharp before each return to G. Then there's a passing chord on A-minor—actually a complex two-step cluster of ninths (she's fond of ninths and elevenths) that halts the song for a moment, as though the narrator, the guy hanging around the Pretenders' sound check, is gathering the courage to speak. After a quick jump up to C-major, the band drops a half-step back to B7, which is, of course, a "Beatles chord" only in the way "Talk of the Town" uses it.

Dominant seventh chords are tantalizing by nature. They want to resolve, and this one does, to E-minor, B7's natural landing spot when the key is G-major. But the verse never returns to G-major itself—the longing she sings will never resolve. Instead, it passes lightly but purposefully through a series of chords that lead organically to others, which in turn suggest still others: *the natural order*. When the vocals start in with: "Such a drag to want something, sometimes. One thing leads to another, I know," the lyric exactly describes the quality of the chord progression. The kid at the sound check, who is the narrator, "wanted you for mine. You arrived like a day, and passed like a cloud," as the chords pass by, changing shape and depth like clouds. It's a brilliant marriage of form and content. Finally, the kid "made a wish. I said it out loud; aloud in a crowd," and as he makes this wish the chords bounce between C and D three times, mounting wishful momentum toward their natural promise of resolving to G. Meanwhile, Farndon's bass pulls the line taut, sliding downward (C-B-A) in the measure between the C and D chords. But the resolution doesn't occur. Just as the title is sung—"It was the talk of the town" (an irony: the "town" scarcely knows he exists)—the song returns to that passing A-minor chord and then commences the second verse on B7, the pivot on which the whole song turns, and the reason she could claim that "I wrote the song around that."[5]

Yet the longing in the second verse appears to be reversed, and thus doubled. "It's not my place to know what you feel," says a new narrator: the singer herself, or someone like her. She's thinking of him in retrospect as she writes the lyrics; as the longing doubles, so does the time and place. She wants to know more about this kid she always ignores. "Who were you then? Who are you now?" She imagines he's a "common laborer by night, by day highbrow"—presumably because he's going to her band's sound checks rather than hitting the pubs. She goes back to her room, looks out the window at the sky, and sees the clouds passing by—the same clouds that reminded him of her. They share them, and they share the longing, that feeling as shapely and hollow as clouds, which "rearrange like the talk of the town" into the title of the song.

And then the payoff. "Talk of the Town" returns to its original G-major vamp, repeating the G-C pattern of the intro. This turns out to have been the chorus, or the closest thing the song has to a chorus (she still wasn't writing them consistently). "Maybe tomorrow, maybe someday": the return to G-major finally pins the longing to the song's tonic resting place, which the bass still doesn't leave even on the following C-major chord, and her voice tumbles down the scale note by note ("*to-mo-o-o-o-orrow*"), as though falling with a long and longing sigh onto the pillow, or more deeply in love. The line is repeated, forcing the listener to appreciate the steep vocal difficulty of the run down the scale on "*to-mo-o-o-o-o-row*," and the next is literally echoed: "You've changed (*you've changed*) your place in this world." The doubled "you've changed" suggests that both admirer and admired, rocker and fan, are singing the line to each other.

The third verse suggests a return to the kid's voice, but it could conceivably still be hers. Part of the genius of "Talk of the Town" is that it can legitimately be heard both ways—not only because of its careful indeterminacy, but also because Chrissie Hynde knew both sides of this longing: she had hung around outside Ziggy Stardust's sound check in the Cleveland cold in 1972, and probably other sound checks too. She can say in either voice: "Oh, but it's hard to live by the rules. I never could and still never do." When "I watch you, still"—getting the most out of the double meaning of "still"—"from a distance, then go back to my room," the image is of singer and fan gazing at one another at a remove after the sound check, wondering what could be, what never will be, what never was. The song ends, appropriately, back on A-minor, hanging unresolved like a cloud yet to pass, a kid left outside a sound check, or a songwriter unsure if she's said all there is to say.

There's a reason a guy was always hanging around the Pretenders' sound checks: they were suddenly one of the hottest bands in England. *Pretenders* went to the top of the charts there in early 1980. Pete Townshend told a radio interviewer that the album was "like a drug." The Pretenders opened for the Who in St. Louis in April 1980. They spent most of 1979 and 1980 touring England and Scotland, playing over a hundred dates, including George Harrison's star-studded benefit Concert for Kampuchea. It took her a long time to arrive at her mystery achievement, but when she finally did, it was the very highest.

America had to be curious about its unknown expat who had taken her game overseas. The Pretenders' first US gig was on March 19, 1980, in Pittsburgh, not far from her old stomping grounds in

Ohio, and the site of her first encounter with Ray Davies, whom she'd soon meet again. The band landed on the cover of *Rolling Stone* in May, treated to a lavish feature by rock writer Kurt Loder. When they played a club in Westchester County, New York—just their tenth American gig—attendees included guitarists Mick Ronson (Ziggy's erstwhile Spider from Mars) and Lenny Kaye (a music writer whom she had known a little in London, and also Patti Smith's guitarist). The Pretenders played a handful of dates in the US, went to Paris for a few days to play there, traveled on to Stockholm—a city that would play a significant role in her career much later—and then went back to the US for a proper, full tour of the country. During a multishow stay in New York City in September 1980, she arranged to meet Ray Davies through an acquaintance, after multiple prior attempts to come face to face with him. The mutual attraction was instant, but two weeks later she and the Pretenders went back to England, where they played sixteen October shows before settling down in London to return to the studio with Chris Thomas.

Overeager to cash in on their success, the Pretenders' management threw together an EP of two new songs the band had recorded for their planned sophomore LP—"Message of Love" and "Talk of the Town"—plus a couple of outtakes from their debut, and one live cut. It was bluntly titled *Extended Play* to help Americans understand a format largely unfamiliar to them at the time (and perhaps because the Pretenders were focused on making a full album and lacked the energy or attention to name a mere and probably unnecessary stopgap).

Pretenders II followed *Extended Play* just two months later, appropriating "Message of Love" and "Talk of the Town" from the EP. The band's name was rendered on the jacket in the same neo-Art Deco font used for *Pretenders*; but the cover also gave the foursome an extra spiffing up, an airbrushing, and moody lighting—not their style at all. No wonder they look so glumly uncomfortable. Their leader was dressed up in a white ruffled blouse under a white couture lady's blazer, with carefully done hair and makeup fit for a model. Although she'd later dabble in such finery, the getup did not fit the thrift store–based, leather-and-jeans fashion she had already invented for herself. If she was "gonna use my style," this was not it.

The remarkable thing was that she already had one. Chrissie Hynde's image is almost as instantly recognizable as her voice. The voice came to her naturally, but the image was much more carefully cultivated and maintained. "How you present yourself to your fellow man is a way of communicating ideas," she writes in *Reckless*, and her use of "man" in that sentence reveals more than it perhaps intends: she usually dresses like our conventional idea of one. But this is not so much to communicate a deliberate androgyny, like David Bowie's, as it is to hearken back to her musical roots: she wants to look the way her band sounds,[6] and the Pretenders Guitar Sound is traditionally "male," even macho.

Arriving in London in the early seventies, she experimented with Vivienne Westwood's zipper-and-bondage chic at Sex, but it didn't really suit her (there is a hilarious anecdote in *Reckless* of a bathroom stall fiasco in a sweaty rubber skirt). Eventually, probably in no small part because she had so little money in her early London years, she abandoned the prevailing fashion and pieced together a style from the men she liked to look at: the get-down boys, the bikers, even the folksingers. She always hated "the little girls in their underwear thing."[7]

In her gender crossover, she bore superficial resemblance to Patti Smith, but Smith influenced neither the Pretenders' music nor their leader's look. Smith was a New York bohemian, a *poète maudit* in reclaimed artist-intellectual clothes—nothing at all like Chrissie Hynde, who was a staunch, straightforward rock-and-roller out of the Midwest in self-imposed London exile, appropriating English dress and custom (she became fond of proper English tea, too). There was really no mold for her. If she has any forebear at all, it might be the relatively unappreciated Suzi

Quatro, another expatriate Midwestern rocker in England. "Chrissie Hynd" interviewed Quatro for *NME*—in a public bathroom—when Quatro was at the height of her British popularity in the early seventies. Quatro had the leather, a manly bass guitar, and a trio of men behind her. But Quatro was ultimately glam in both image and sound, favoring jumpsuits and T. Rex, and although the Pretenders came later, their musical influences were of an older vintage. Naturally, so were the clothes that expressed them.

The abiding image of Chrissie Hynde: tight jeans and tall boots, oversized men's blazers and low-knotted neckties, chains more than necklaces, vests with no shirt underneath, simple muscle tees emblazoned with attention-getting images or slogans; one commentator described her as "Keith Richards's kid sister."[8] A little lace might peek out at the wrists, but mainly just to offset the leather (which the animal rights zealot no longer acquires; the now-iconic red leather jacket she wore on the cover of *Pretenders* has been bequeathed to the Rock and Roll Hall of Fame). Her only noticeable makeup—and it's unmissable, her signature detail—has always been the heavy black eyeliner, which never fails to ring her eyes. She looks as strange without it as Elvis Costello does without his glasses. The eyeliner gives her a sleepless or vaguely criminal look, like that of an addict or a bandit. Down into these kohl-ringed eyes encroach her low-hanging bangs; she has a near get-down boy cut on the cover of *Pretenders*. She has occasionally grown her hair out a little or worn it a bit shorter, but she's gone to the same cheap London stylist for years, and the essential do hasn't changed since at least 1978: straight but coarse, and deliberately unkempt, with a hank or two often sticking out behind her.

What completes the picture is a guitar: the ultimate signifier of rock authenticity. She has always been, above all, a rock and roll rhythm guitarist in a really good band with a commitment to strong live performance. The togs are merely a pose without the music, and she detests poseurs; but the guitar itself is part of the pose—a rock and roll garment, not merely a rock and roll instrument. Her sound and image go together, seamlessly, incomparably. She has no real peers—not Joan Jett, who was too metal, and not Stevie Nicks, who was too witchy—and no true heirs: Sheryl Crow is too mainstream; Liz Phair is too sexed up; avowed adorer Shirley Manson of Garbage doesn't play an instrument.

Because so few women have fronted their own rock bands, there haven't been many appropriate ears for the advice Chrissie Hynde gave rock-chick hopefuls in 1994, when "Women in Rock" had finally caught up with her and wanted to sit at her feet and learn what to put on theirs: "Remember, you're in a rock and roll band. It's not f— me, it's f— you."[9] The advice may be sound, but there's no use trying to emulate her. No one else ever has. She is singular, a solitaire in the rock pantheon.

That *Pretenders II* was not as well received as *Pretenders* is hardly a surprise; follow-ups to sensational debuts tend to suffer by comparison, especially when the main songwriter has to rush to compose new material after a grinding year-plus on the road. (Unsurprisingly, her plans to write the album's songs while on tour didn't pan out.) Yet it's a very good record, in the same mold as *Pretenders* and with highlights every bit its equal. It uses many of the same ingredients to even stronger, if not always greater, effect: *Pretenders II* is more astringent—nastier in some places, tenderer in others. It winnows the substance of *Pretenders* down to more concentrated if less juicy essences, the sound of an already strong, confident band growing even stronger and more confident.

Its first two songs update the progress of the debut's female rake. "Precious" becomes "The Adultress," which takes the animating lawlessness of "Precious" to its logical extreme: the narrator commits "the worst crime in history" in the role of the unsavory Other Woman (which she "didn't want to be") in "Private Life." Over an angular and angry guitar riff, she meets her lover in the park, and he takes her into the woods for a tumble. But she takes no pride in being his mistress; she ends up drowning her sorrows in a bar.

The next tune, "Bad Boys Get Spanked," comes out of the gate sounding a bit like "Tattooed Love Boys," a sort of dominatrix-rockabilly groove with Shootout at the OK Corral sonic effects, but it quickly flips the script on her attackers: "You're not supposed to do that. You know you're not allowed to." She is in charge now, and she is making no new concessions to the radio her band has conquered. Where she "had to fuck off" in "Precious," now to her vanquished adversary she administers lashings of both whip and tongue: "Shit on that!" and "You don't listen, do you, asshole?" She concludes "Bad Boys Get Spanked" not with her trademark *Ohhhhhhhhh!* but with a caterwaul version of it—not vulnerable but wild, piercing, and savage.

As on the debut, *Pretenders II* waits until its third track to widen its attitude and musical range, and it does so by reaching way back. "Message of Love" borrows its title from one of her favorite sources, Jimi Hendrix (two of whose songs would appear on Pretenders albums in the next decade), and its sentiment from Wayne Fontana and the Mindbenders, who sang in 1965: "The purpose of a man is to love a woman, and the purpose of a woman is to love a man."[10] "Message of Love" softens much of the damage done by "The Adultress" and "Bad Boys Get Spanked." A funky, loose shuffle (it feels like it has a ghost of reggae in it), supplies a vibe that is generous and warm: "The reason we're here as man and woman is to love each other, take care of each other," she croons. Having introduced love into the conversation, she ups the literary ante, quoting Oscar Wilde's *Lady Windermere's Fan*: "We are all of us in the gutter, but some of us are looking at the stars." The verse gives way to an almost sweetly melodic valentine in the chorus (it sounds like something Ray Davies could have written), with the boys in the band *ooh-we-oohing* in the background as she sings, right out of fifties doo-wop:

Me and you,
Every night, every day,
We'll be together always this way.
Your eyes are blue like the heavens above.
Talk to me, darlin', with a message of love.

That last line is a clever inversion. The song, itself a message of love, is asking for one in return.

The next song makes the same request, in effect. "I Go to Sleep" is another Kinks cover, but only barely: the Kinks never recorded it except as a demo, although versions of it appeared in 1965 by both Cher and Peggy Lee (and later by others). It's another lullaby, this one in waltz time: "I go to sleep and imagine that you're there with me." Chrissie Hynde uses Ray Davies's own words to send a message of love to him—and there's a message of love in her very choice of such an obscure cover: she's letting him know that her attention is keen and close, that she knows his catalogue through and through. It wasn't the first message she'd sent him. She'd written him an open love letter in *NME* as "Chrissie Hynd" in 1974, reviewing the Kinks song "Mirror of Love" (an oddly similar title to "Message of Love"): "Raymond Douglas Davies is the only songwriter I can think of who can write such personal material (and he is always *very* personal) and never get embarrassing. One of the true romantics of our time."[11] She made a wish, said it out loud. And now that she had met him, it was coming true.

Musically, "I Go to Sleep" is really just a trial run for its follow-up, "Birds of Paradise," also a waltzing lullaby. Many years later, in 2014, she was asked by an interviewer if she had considered doing an album of ballads. "No one wants to hear that shit from me," she shot back. "This is supposed to be a rock band." It's a shame she never embraced the idea (although balladry does crop up on all of her albums). She had the voice for it, and the songwriting chops.

"Birds of Paradise" is a gorgeous composition and vocal performance: a "sing-songy, fetching piece of intimacy about lost childhood ideals," as the musician-writer Scott Miller puts it.[12] Lilting, tender, and sweetly mournful, it's a letter to an old friend: "When I was a little girl with clay horses and lambs on the shelf, I caught frogs in ditches, listened for elves. My friends and I had a world unto ourselves." Here again are her commitments to sanctuaries, for both children and animals. The singer and her friend are nestled in their world as "two birds of paradise," but they know they'll have to leave the nest someday: "Nothing lasts forever," the friend warns her, in tears. The singer herself seems to have done something to hasten the demise of their childhood innocence: "Please forgive me," she begs—perhaps for becoming a rock star, both singer and sinner. She writes her friend letters from hotel rooms in Stockholm and Rome, where she's living "the life they say that dreams are made of," but the childhood dream is the one she still longs for. It's one of her most affecting vocal performances, especially coming as soon as it does after the snarling "Adultress" and "Bad Boys Get Spanked." And it one-ups Davies himself, taking the dream of "I Go to Sleep" and outdreaming it, making of the solitary and wishful "I imagine that you're there with me" an almost brazen invitation: "Come into my dream and dream with me."

"Talk of the Town" closes side one, and side two relights the fire with the ruthless and pointed "Pack It Up," a bruising rocker that both opens and closes with the shouted insult: "You guys are the pits of the world!" She took this line almost verbatim from a highly publicized on-court outburst by the tennis star John McEnroe, whom the Pretenders had befriended in New York. "I walked straight into the vocal booth and started the song with it. John thanked me for it later. Apparently, it cheered him up after getting fined $1,500." (So, perhaps, did the marijuana she claimed to have shared with him during Wimbledon in the eighties: "He would always call me because he knew I had pot.")[13]

Although "I don't do sports," she announced, she and McEnroe seemed to be kindred spirits in many ways. "Being on tour sends me crazy," she said. "I drink too much and out comes the John McEnroe in me."[14] They have had very similar careers in their different milieus. Both enjoyed rocket-to-the-top success in the early eighties as brash but very artistic punks, going straight to No. 1; both married rock stars (McEnroe's wife, Patty Smyth, whose band Scandal scored a few hits, owed Chrissie Hynde an image and career debt); both fell into fallow periods marred by injury and self-destructiveness; both staged successful comebacks by broadening their craft and attentions (McEnroe became a world-class doubles player and the flag bearer for America's Davis Cup team). Much later she invited him, a fairly serious guitar player who had briefly had his own band, to play on one of the songs on her solo debut, *Stockholm*—which happens to be the city where McEnroe's most famous midmatch tantrum took place in 1984.

"Pack It Up" makes a slight return to Cleveland, à la "Precious." "Burning down the Innerbelt" is a reference to a Cleveland bridge, and "I'm burning every bridge," she vows. Then she zeroes in on Nick Lowe, or in any case the category of man he represents. "Pack It Up" was the first of the explicitly personal attacks she has regularly written and recorded throughout her career. Sometimes she goes after specific offenders: Michael Jackson, for example, in 1986's "How Much Did You Get for Your Soul?," and the deadbeat dad of that same year's "Chill Factor," who is almost certainly her absent husband Jim Kerr. Or she can be suggestive, as in 1999's "Popstar," which may refer to any wannabe chick rocker who "wants to move a million units," but could specifically mean the woman with whom the deadbeat dad ended up, Patsy Kensit, best known as an actress, who had pop music pretensions. (Thus the song takes aim at the deadbeat dad by association.) In "Dark Sunglasses," from *Stockholm* (2014), she targets a preening rock and roll has-been, with specific enough ammunition to aim at a particular guy but not enough to name him. Most often, though, she sings from a broader rancor, as in her constant scorn for the One Percent (a phrase she used in a lyric long before the Occupy movement popularized it) in songs like "Middle of the Road," "Millionaires," and "Fools Must Die": "the world rejoices when they stumble to the ground." It's in songs like these that her humorlessness does her few favors.

"Pack It Up" succeeds by compiling in an increasingly loopy and comical list of the offenses of Nick Lowe and his ilk: "Your insipid record collection! That dumb home video center! The usual pornography." But most of the rest of *Pretenders II* is laden with bitter invective. "Waste Not Want Not," a reggae tune, is a jeremiad about environmental destruction, political corruption, and other ills, but it connects them to her originating concerns: "You slaughter when you feast, you disrespect the beast." And there's a reference to "sacred cows," invoking her lifelong Hinduism. Carnivorousness connects to many kinds of destruction and cruelty inflicted by gluttonous, rapacious fat cats who "take, take, take what you don't need" and are guilty of "a golden harvest reaped without intelligence." They've built "a network of concrete and steel" in which not only the animals but "all the children in god's kingdom bleed," and they've left us "a future that's void of the beauty and the majesty that life on Earth is meant to be." When the Earth Mother derides "car culture," she means all of this: unlivable cities, lifeless countryside; despoliation, ecological ruin, and humanitarian catastrophe.

From "Waste Not Want Not" to the end of *Pretenders II*, the songs go through "the war waging endlessly" in "Day after Day" (with a monitory glimpse of dolphins, presumably endangered, in the sea); "Jealous Dogs" who'll "take your back and leave your shirt" (including a "jealous bitch" in high heels who's "always wanting more") and treat you "like some kind of dog food"; and, in the heavy, magnetic "English Roses," "fruit cut from the vine, forgot and left to rot"—these darling buds are metaphors for "girls next door" who are seduced and abandoned. The sentiment is generally dark, but the band is in fine form on the second side of *Pretenders II*, melding propulsive muscular grooves to inventive but subtle changes in chords, keys, and musical moods. It all sounds intuitive, unforced, whereas *Pretenders* sometimes sounded breathless and willful and jagged. Even the vocals on *Pretenders II* offer a few surprises: her spoken-word lines on "Day after Day"; the canine yelps on "Jealous Dogs." Chris Thomas's sonic layering, especially in guitar treatments and overdubs, adds complexity and depth to the music without calling attention to itself—it's all in service to her songs. Meanwhile, Thomas and Jimmy Scott confidently purvey the deceptively complex and accomplished Pretenders Guitar Sound, including a few searing, compressed solos.

Scott was just coming into his own as a guitar great. None of the band's enduring hits are on side two of *Pretenders II* (although "Pack It Up" still featured in live Chrissie Hynde sets as late as 2014), but the songs show the Pretenders in strong command as they rock to the album's surprisingly buoyant closing number, cheekily entitled "Louie Louie." It's a soul rave-up that hearkens back to her early music loves; the two-chord vamp echoes the similarly upbeat album-closer of *Pretenders*, "Mystery Achievement"; and it pays homage to the Kingsmen's garage-rock original. The joyful tune brings in a horn section, and the boys sing a vocal part of their own during the drum break. The song's encouraging message is that rock and roll will never die, at least not in good hands like the Pretenders'.

Ironic, given what was to come next.

In support of the release of *Pretenders II*, the band went on a world tour from June 1981 through March 1982, playing over a hundred shows on four continents. The sets generally comprised the same fifteen songs from the Pretenders' first two albums, with slight variations and occasional covers of older songs like "(Your Love Keeps Lifting Me) Higher and Higher" and "Money (That's What I Want)." The consistency of the selections and the sequencing allowed the band to grow into a tight, accomplished unit behind its strong leader—or so it seemed. In reality, they were unraveling.

Whatever drug dependency Farndon and Scott were experiencing—Farndon appears to have been the worse abuser, or in any case less able to handle the drugs—the tour probably deepened it: the Pretenders wasted no time in embracing the sex-and-drugs cliché that has undone so many rock bands. Farndon's demeanor and playing were worsening along with his heroin addiction, and any fallout from his terminated romance with his bandleader grew more toxic on tour as she carried on her courtship with Ray Davies. The others in the band did not get on well with Davies, who was a self-possessed, sometimes presumptive sort. Jealousy, fatigue, addiction, and tension mounted as the Pretenders circled the globe in uncomfortably close travel quarters. Those tensions may have worsened Farndon's heroin abuse, and, in a vicious cycle, his heroin abuse fed tensions back into the band.

It wasn't just Farndon who was in freefall. Scott, "a speed freak" since before Chrissie Hynde met him, was availing himself of copious amounts of drugs. The Pretenders' fearless leader wasn't doing much better. She was literally kicking and screaming her way across America. Hanging out at a club in Memphis, she took offense to being asked, in crude hands-on style, to clear an aisle. When she just as crudely refused, she was kicked out, then arrested, and she bashed out the police car window with her boot. In New York she crashed a Johnny Thunders show and, as she remembered it, "ended up on the floor of the stage crying and calling the audience complacent hippies." It was a telling commentary on her state of mind, body, and soul when after the show, Thunders, the crown prince of smacked-out punk basket cases, sporting a swollen purple lip from falling down a flight of stairs, told her she needed to get her act together.

Later in the Pretenders' tour, in a hotel room in Philadelphia, the generally steady Martin Chambers suffered a fit of anger—which was now the dominant feeling in the band. He punched a lamp, shattering it and slicing a tendon in his hand. Most of the next month's shows had to be canceled. When he could play regularly again, the Pretenders resumed the final leg of a tour that had taken them to America and back twice, and now flung them all the way to the other side of the world, where they played Japan and Australia. Before the encore of a show in Melbourne, Farndon lit a cigarette backstage, and an elderly custodian told him smoking wasn't allowed. Farndon responded by punching him in the face. The other three band members exchanged a look that confirmed what they'd all been thinking: they were going to get through the dregs of their tour—a grim show in Bangkok in April 1982—and then kick him out of the band.

Almost immediately upon arriving back home in England, Chrissie Hynde got pregnant with Ray Davies. Two months later, in June, she shared the happy news with Scott and Chambers, who congratulated her. Then they agreed to have Dave Hill, their manager, tell Farndon he was out of the Pretenders.

Two days later, Hill called her to report that her bandmate had ODed and died. Not Pete Farndon. Jimmy Scott. He had done too much cocaine, and it stopped his heart. He was twenty-five.

The shock had layers. It was not just that a band member had died, and not just that Jimmy had died. It was that Pete was the one who hadn't seemed long for this world. And he wasn't. Less than a year later, Farndon died of a heroin overdose. His mother thought his dismissal from the Pretenders had led to his addiction. She had to listen to his ex-lover and ex-bandleader tell her that it was the other way around.

Until *Reckless* was published as she turned sixty-four, Chrissie Hynde never spoke much about her bandmates' deaths, and even in her memoir she seems to withhold nearly as much as she divulges. She mostly ignores her romance with Farndon, and she condemns his drugging and its related behavior while eliding Scott's substance abuse; in the epilogue, Scott is portrayed angelically. Perhaps her most eloquent tribute to the two of them, other than the songs she wrote in Scott's honor and her long dedication to maintaining his Pretenders Guitar Sound, was the brief eulogy, almost an epitaph, that she delivered as part of the Pretenders' Rock and Roll Hall of Fame induction speech in 2005: "Without them we wouldn't be here," she said. But then she added, with her trademark laconic wit: "On the other hand, without us they might have been here. But that's the way it works in rock and roll."[15]

Although she made a full artistic recovery after their deaths, one element of her music was permanently reduced: live performance. After Farndon and Scott were gone, the Pretenders' subsequent touring career was generally sporadic and in short bursts; there was only one more full-year-on-the-road expedition, in 1984. With the exception of Martin Chambers's occasional returns to the drum kit, no other memberships in the band seemed entirely certified save Chrissie Hynde's.

Many longstanding rock acts build an evolving, even dynamic relationship to their songs over years of playing them live, as well as a relationship to their fans, who in turn expand their own relationship to the songs by witnessing performances of them. But the deaths of Farndon and Scott, along with Chrissie Hynde's long layoffs to raise her children, deprived the Pretenders of substantially extending these relationships. It's a shame, because she has always been an excellent live frontwoman. She is naturally charismatic; if indeed "confidence was a bluff," as she writes in *Reckless*, she's a great bluffer on stage. Into her sixties, she can still draw a respectable and ebullient crowd and give them a high-energy set; her songs show well live and have nearly always been played by a formidable, engaging lineup of Pretenders behind her.

From childhood, she had a long, rich steeping in the rock music tradition and could have played across a range of styles, from covers to reimagined versions of her own songs. But, save for the 1995 Pretenders-with-strings experiment, *The Isle of View*, the Pretenders' live performances never tinkered much with the songs themselves. They played the songs mostly straight, as studio versions come to life, more to confirm the songs than to recolor them. Nor were covers (other than those previously recorded on studio albums) an appreciable part of the band's sets. From 1984 on, the Pretenders' live act was mostly a respectable formality, less an organic part of the band's life—not least because half of its foundation was dead.

With that half gone and a baby in her arms, she could easily have taken the path of Edie Brickell, another charismatic lead singer with an idiosyncratic voice who fronted a popular but short-lived band backed by men, and who met an older, legendary musician in New York (Paul Simon) and sacrificed her stardom and most of her career to become his wife and the mother of his children. But if 1973 was the year Chrissie Hynde launched her rock and roll dream in London, and if 1979 was the year that dream came true, then 1983, despite and perhaps fueled by its tumult and grief, was the year that brought that dream to life—real life. She regrouped and made the album that established her as a permanent rock and roll force.

FOUR

TIME THE AVENGER

Learning to Crawl

> A *labour of love, labour of love,*
> *The torment, the worry and woe.*
> *Love's full of fears, bruises and tears:*
> *That's the way that a true love grows*

> —THE KINKS, "LABOUR OF LOVE," *STATE OF CONFUSION*, 1983

When Chrissie Hynde first met Ray Davies in 1980, the first word out of her mouth was "Hello." He thought she was saying, "Help me."

"She couldn't take the sudden fame that had come to her," Davies later recalled, "and I think she saw me as someone who had done all that rock 'n' roll stuff and understood it."[1]

A well-worn cliché lurks here, with vaguely sexist undertones, or a touch of *Pygmalion* in any case: wild chick rocker can't handle the life; she keeps boozing and brawling until she meets an older, more cultured English gentleman who gives her manners and motherhood. Davies writes:

[Arista Records executive Bob] Feiden took us both out to dinner at a swanky midtown restaurant. Chrissie must have been eating bad road food at the time, because she not only scoffed down her meal but seemed to enjoy it so much that she innocently mopped up the remains of her food with a piece of bread. Quite acceptable behavior in my opinion, particularly after being subject to road food for months on end, but as we walked home, Bob took me to one side and whispered firmly in my ear: "She's a great singer, an emerging talent, and quite possibly a Grammy winner, but with table manners like that she is definitely not for you."[2]

Their relationship lasted less than four years, but it's one of the great superstar love pairings in rock history. Both are Hall of Famers, beloved and revered. Both are articulate and have given plenty of time to the media over the years, despite their shared aversion to the necessary publicity and self-revelation that accompanies stardom. Yet they have seldom spoken on the record about each other. It isn't clear whether their mutual silence comes from an explicit agreement, instinctive avoidance of a perhaps painful subject, or a natural commitment to protecting their child, but more than thirty years of restraint evinces an abiding desire for privacy.

Davies has published both an autobiography and a memoir, but Chrissie Hynde is completely absent from the first book and appears on a grand total of six pages of *Americana* (2013), his recollection of life in the United States. She has been even more tight-lipped about their relationship. Since their breakup in 1984, she doesn't seem to have spoken about him in an interview even once. *Reckless* gives him not much more than a page—whether this is by her choice or by his request ultimately makes no difference—and manages to skip from the beginning to the end of the relationship in a single sentence almost immediately after introducing him: After an American journalist arranged their first meeting at Trax, an industry-friendly club on New York City's Upper West Side, she writes, "I saw him every day after that, whenever we were in the same town, but we were not suited to each other." The five short paragraphs that follow do little more than summarize three of their embarrassingly public spats in New York—storming out of theaters, throwing gifts out of high hotel windows—before concluding, "Ours was a battle of wills." She wryly captions a happy picture of them in *Reckless*: "Me and Ray. Always laughing."

She has treated the relationship the same way she treated the deaths of Pete Farndon and Jimmy Scott: with the dignity of silence wherever possible, and with a few dry words of explanation when necessary. Her withholding of evidence and testimony is an essential part of Chrissie Hynde's biography: her guardedness and privacy, the firm line she has long sought to draw between the limelight and the nightlight. She is by no means resistant to exposure: she's a generous, entertaining live performer and a voluble, forthcoming interviewee when she chooses to be, and she isn't at all shy about amplifying her celebrity for the animal rights cause. But she seldom consents to extraneous attention, and there are few rock stars of her stature who put on fewer airs. Some of the tremendous respect she has earned over the years, especially from her peers, may come partly from her rigorously maintained authenticity as a public figure. Chrissie Hynde seems like an actual person even when she's playing rock star. There's something very true about her, and much of it inheres precisely in her protection of the truth about her.

That protection includes the truth about Chrissie Hynde and Ray Davies. They were not a public rock-star couple. They didn't even record or perform together except in a handful of Kinks concerts at which she made impromptu appearances during encores, which apparently enraged Davies's brother Dave, the Kinks' guitarist, who never needed much provocation to get into his next row with Ray. The couple's lone recorded collaboration didn't come about until 2009, a quarter century after they split up. Davies had written a Christmastime duet, "Postcard from London," although not with his ex in mind. "She wasn't my first choice," Davies writes. "I wanted Dame Vera Lynn, because the song has the sort of melody that she would handle rather well." But Lynn, ninety-two years old, wasn't available, and Natalie Hynde—not Natalie Davies—persuaded her father and mother to collaborate on the song. They consented, but only on the grounds that they record their parts separately. "Chrissie came into the studio and did her bit brilliantly," Davies allows, but then adds: "I wasn't there at the time." (He has also given a slightly different, and much chillier, account: that he watched her record her part from behind a one-way mirror.) He also went out of his way to deny any warm sentiment or nostalgia: "It wasn't recorded around a log fire or anything. We weren't toasting marshmallows and cracking nuts. My girlfriend Karen sang on the demo."[3]

Chrissie Hynde and Davies are very similar in many ways. Both come from working-class backgrounds they were eager to escape. Both have brothers who are also musicians. Both are notoriously combative characters who can sing both sweetly and savagely, whose fiery pugnacity conceals a deep well of romanticism from which have come some arrestingly tender, revealing songs. Both exude a pronounced yet slightly overperformed Englishness, she as an acolyte and adopter of London, he (so the story goes) because he and the Kinks were banned from the United States at the height of their popularity and had to retreat behind the fey, forced Britannia of albums like *The Village Green Preservation Society* and *Arthur*. (But are "Wicked Annabella" and the derisive putdown "People Take Pictures of Each Other" really so fey?) Both were immensely famous for a few years; neither quite returned to those heights of stardom. They achieved and maintained much of their emeritus status through longevity and personal charisma, not via the pop charts, where neither was much of a presence after age forty.

They planned to get married and to conceive a child on their wedding night. "It was so *romantic*," Hynde told *Rolling Stone*, not long before the couple broke up, as it turned out. But they didn't get married. "Ray and I had a row, and when we got down to the registry office, the guy took one look at us and refused to marry us."[4]

Davies has given a similar account of their aborted marriage plans, but it sounds fishy, romanticized—even though, as *Rolling Stone* reported, "exactly nine months after the reluctant registrar turned the couple away, Chrissie gave birth to a baby girl,"[5] just as they had planned. Ray was there at the delivery. But why didn't they settle the dustup during the pregnancy and get married some other day? Is the making of lifelong vows by two intelligent people deeply in love, both of them in their thirties, a now-or-never proposition? It sounds like a pat, possibly glib story they've agreed to tell in order to withhold the truth, which is probably more complicated and contradictory than they've allowed it to appear on the record. Perhaps the truth lurks on other records: their own. Davies has acknowledged that his song "Animal" (one of the last the Kinks ever recorded) is about their relationship. Although they had "sunsets on the sands, holding onto caring hands . . . there were vampire fangs as the angels sang," the song goes, and "broken bottles and abuse." Some of the abuse was verbal: "There were terrible long-distance fights. The phone was our worst enemy," Davies told an interviewer in 1987, in one of his few concessions to the press about their relationship.[6]

Another of Davies's songs offers an additional explanation. "Labour of Love," from the Kinks' *State of Confusion*—released in 1983 as the relationship was unraveling—works the stress of impending parenthood into its very title, plus a hint of the couple's separate (and separating) career commitments. The song begins with a prefatory anarchic guitar rendition of "Here Comes the Bride" (it evokes Jimi Hendrix's version of the "Star Spangled Banner"). Then it launches into a driving, sneering rock song:

> *Marriage is a two-headed transplant.*
> *Sometimes that's how it seems.*
> *When the sex wears off, it's all give and take,*
> *And it's goodbye to all your dreams.*

She was not so candid in her music. *Learning to Crawl*, also released in 1983, is not a relationship album—or rather, it's about the relationship between mother and child, and between woman and the world, not between woman and man. It's the Pretenders' most accomplished and fully realized album: concise, confident, and polished, achieved without half the band's founding members but preserving—perhaps even perfecting—what they had given to it. "One of the things that kept the band alive, ironically, was the death of Jimmy Scott. I felt I couldn't let the music die when he did. We'd worked too hard to get it up to where it was. I had to finish what we started."[7]

Scott had left her a usable legacy. When the Pretenders returned from their world tour in early 1982, Scott not only wanted to fire Pete Farndon; he also wanted to add another guitarist, Robbie McIntosh, whose playing he knew well. Instead McIntosh assumed Scott's role as smoothly as anyone could be expected to under the circumstances, and he brought with him bassist Malcolm Foster. Billy Bremner, a longtime Nick Lowe collaborator whom Scott also admired, played guitar on some of the early recording sessions for *Learning to Crawl*. So did bassist Tony Butler, who was well known from the popular Scottish band Big Country.

The most important contributor was the man who had been there all along, producer Chris Thomas—"the Fifth Pretender," as even the band had come to think of him by the time they had finished recording *Pretenders II*. When the new combo recorded *Learning to Crawl*, it was Thomas who had the idea to set them up in the studio as though they were playing live, the setting where she and Martin Chambers felt most comfortable, the drug-addled shows of the previous tour's latter dates notwithstanding.[8] It was Thomas who knew how to layer McIntosh's guitar parts the way Scott had layered his, preserving and in some cases improving the Pretenders Guitar Sound. Perhaps most crucially, it was Thomas who knew how to coax a vocal performance out of his famously shy, sometimes uncooperative singer. "When it came to her vocals, Chrissie was great so long as nobody else was in the room," recalled Steve Churchyard, the engineer for the *Learning to Crawl* sessions. "The band, everybody, was kicked out. They all went upstairs and played pool, and nobody was allowed to come back down until we'd got [the vocals recorded]. On a vocal day we might sit around for hours and drink tea and have lunch and chat about everything other than what we were about to do, and then at a certain point— which was part of [Thomas's] gift as a producer—he would say, 'OK, how about now?'"[9]

Thomas's production of *Learning to Crawl* boasts pop sheen without slickness: a bigger, more reverberant sound than he had created for the Pretenders' first two albums, suited to the larger venues they'd soon be playing, joining the mainstream without pandering to it. The mix puts Chrissie Hynde's lead vocals squarely front and center. Thomas's production approach was entirely in the service of her songwriting, which had achieved new levels of maturity, power, and economy. As a lyricist, she was reaching deeper while growing at once more nuanced and more direct, both wiser and more vulnerable. There was greater musicality as well. She no longer trafficked in her "treacherously erratic meter" and hissed profanities, or came on raw and punk. The melodist Jimmy Scott had uncloseted was not going back into hiding, although she did not outright abandon her original style and attitude. There are still conspicuous chord and key changes on *Learning to Crawl*, as well as shots of her trademark spitfire, but she began to deploy them with more craft, subtlety, and deliberation. And although she had learned how to write catchy choruses and bridges, as the classic single "Back on the Chain Gang" proves, she did not always do so. Most of the songs on *Learning to Crawl* do not have bridges.

The album's title needs little explanation, voicing as it does an obvious and tidy double entendre about child-rearing and falling to the floor in the wake of tragedy: on the cover, the band members (now including McIntosh and Foster) are photographed wearing black. "Back on the Chain Gang," *Learning to Crawl*'s signature song and the first one written and recorded for the album, does require an asterisk, however. It is generally assumed that the song was written as an elegy to Jimmy Scott, but she had already composed and even played it for him before his death. Later, she acknowledged, the song became about him, although she has not elaborated on what revisions, if any, she made to the lyrics.

In retrospect, a song like that could scarcely be about anyone else even if she didn't change so much as a note. Although the internet hosts a free-floating claim that the song was inspired by a photo of Ray Davies she found in her wallet,[10] it seems unlikely that "Back on the Chain Gang" can be substantially about him; they appeared to be happily coupled (as happily as they ever were, at least) at the time she wrote the tune, probably in 1981 or 1982. Chances are good that "Back on the Chain Gang" was inspired, if not directly then at least emotionally, by the couple she lived with in Paris in 1975, Sasha and the transvestite Sabrina/Sabo. In *Reckless* she describes that short period as the happiest of her life.

"Back on the Chain Gang" is a perfect pop song. It borrows the tried and true old-photograph-of-you trope (as does Jackson Browne's "Fountain of Sorrow") and does something savvy with it: it widens the frame in the second verse to include "circumstance beyond our control"—"the phone, the TV and the news of the world." Private life drama is complicated by, even a symptom of, societal interference, political oppression, and environmental maladies.

The song's chorus deftly plays with the title, posing the chain gang as both the prison penance it is and the back-to-work resolve it could be. With the men in the band grunting in laborious effort during the chorus, the song also evokes the classic "Chain Gang" by Sam Cooke—from whom the Pretenders took their name—and helps set up a later, album-closing reference to another great soul singer, Otis Redding. There's a wish, too, to get "back on the train," that most potent and packed of Chrissie Hynde's lyrical symbols: the train stands for escape, adventure, and a return to an innocent, youthful "place in the past."

The way the bridge modulates from D-major to D-minor—not a

natural change by any means—is a stroke of brilliance: it immediately tows the song into minor-key melancholia just as the lyrical mood descends deeper. "It brings me to my knees"—learning to crawl—"when I see what they've done to you." And when she vows "that the faceless but maleficent "they" will "fall to ruin one day for making us part," the song changes key again, not back to its original D-major but up a full step to E-major, as if emerging onto a higher plateau of understanding and acceptance—even a sort of solemn optimism. "I found a picture of you," she repeats—the classic setup for an epiphany derived from the same source. Her voice reaches its highest, most plaintive note in the song with another wordless, "*Oh, oh-oh-oh, oh-oh*"—another reminder, like "*to-mo-o-o-orrow*" in "Talk of the Town," that she can make deceptively difficult melismatic vocal lines sound effortless. It is a more complex, vulnerable update of the long *Ohhhhhhhhhh!* of the first two Pretenders albums.

"Those were the happiest days of my life," she sings, despite all the pain of their aftermath, teasing out the word "life" for four vibrant, sing-songy syllables. The departed, she realizes, did not die in vain but gave her a profound gift: "a break in the battle." Not merely the battle that pitted her band against the demons of stardom, which the deaths of Scott and Farndon tragically ended, but also a break in the "endless war" she lamented and protested in "Day after Day" on *Pretenders II*. The loved one in the photograph was a bulwark against those very "circumstances beyond our control," sacrificing himself for her by taking all the shrapnel, and all the necessary drugs, to absorb and numb the pain of those circumstances, reversing the role of protector and protected.

"Back on the Chain Gang" was released as a single in 1982, well over a year before *Learning to Crawl* came out. (It also appeared on the soundtrack to the movie *The King of Comedy* in 1983.) The song reached the top ten on the American rock charts and served three notices: first, emphatically, that the Pretenders were not done as a band; second, that their leader was changing and growing as a songwriter; and third, that her tough stance was softening and her picture of the world was widening. (Any of her fans confused or disappointed by this evolution should perhaps have anticipated it from the composer of songs like "Kid," "Waste Not Want Not," and "Birds of Paradise.")

"Back on the Chain Gang" was not the only testimony she gave in the summer of 1982. The single of "Back on the Chain Gang" is backed with the bluesy swamp-rocker "My City Was Gone," which brings her environmental concerns back home and is her first song in the explicit voice of an expatriate. She revisits her hometown—what sounds like, "Hey, ho" is really "A, O": Akron, Ohio—and deplores the collapse of its urban core. "There was no train station," that cardinal symbol of a city's health and solvency (not to mention the romance of the train whistle); "there was no downtown," only "parking spaces": car culture. The surrounding countryside, too, had been "paved down the middle by the government," which was increasingly the target of her wrath. "The farms of Ohio had been replaced by shopping malls," she laments; worst of all, "Muzak filled the air." It's satisfying, if probably a reach, to imagine that Ray Davies had this song in mind when he composed "Come Dancing" for *State of Confusion* in 1982: "They put a parking lot on a piece of land where the local supermarket used to stand." Or perhaps it was the other way around, and she was borrowing from "Come Dancing" when she composed "My City Was Gone."

Learning to Crawl was released in January 1984, just as Chrissie Hynde and Ray Davies were breaking up. The album opens with the propulsive "Middle of the Road"—another double entendre not only announcing the singer's new placement in life but also obliquely lampooning the toothless "Adult Contemporary" radio format, a club of which no self-respecting rocker would want to be a member:

The middle of the road
Is trying to find me.
I'm standing in the middle of life with my pains[11] behind me.
And I got a smile for everyone I meet,
As long as you don't try dragging my bay,
Or dropping the bomb on my street.

The "you" here is not a specific person; it's the military-industrial complex, the same "they" who would "fall to ruin one day" in "Back on the Chain Gang" (and who will absorb more of her invective as her career goes on). But the effects are felt more personally than ever. When she commands, "Don't try . . . dropping the bomb," she means not to drop it "on my street." She's insisting on her individual rights (and she'll still be doing it in "Legalise Me," on 1999's *¡Viva El Amor!*). The entire second verse attacks the rich who make their fortune by exploiting the Third World—"fat guys driving round in jeeps through the city . . . past corrugated tin shacks full up with kids"—but again the exploitation comes right to her neighborhood in the form of fans, autograph hounds, paparazzi, and all the riffraff of the music biz. "The middle of the road is no private cul-de-sac," she sings. "I can't get from the cab to curb without some little jerk on my back."

After "Back on the Chain Gang" echoes the theme of "Middle of the Road"—private life corrupted by "the phone, the TV, and the news of the world"—both "Time the Avenger" and "Watching the Clothes" elaborate on it. The former seems like a straightforward lecture to a well-off but deluded professional man, a Babbitt figure who has left his wife and kids, but the lyrics include new attunements to the complex machinery of power. "You're the best in your field, in your office with your girls and desk and leather chair." These apparently mundane things are actually signifiers of male capitalist privilege, objects in a system of oppression that keeps both money and women in pocket. Thus, when the Babbitt figure's wife inevitably leaves him, his heart may not be hurt, but he'll feel it somewhere more sensitive: his bank account. "With what you'll have left, you'll be forever under pressure to support her." And like his funds, time is always dwindling. One of the teachings of the *Bhagavad Gita*—that the material world is a mirage—informs her lecture: "Nobody's permanent. Everything's on loan here."

"Watching the Clothes"—almost "Washing the Clothes," cleverly, when sung—sounds a bit like what it describes. The beat is straightforward and driving, and the repetitive primary guitar riff and the topsy-turvy chords suggest a spin cycle. It's a song about money and class. On a Saturday night, instead of going out and having fun or getting into a fight—the sorts of things you'd expect from a rock song about this day of the week—the narrator (a waitress, of course) is at the launderette. She's survived another week of "serving the middle class," and the bitter reward is just more servitude: doing her washing. The working class is caught in an endless cycle of drudgery, and the closest approximation of Saturday night TV the narrator can afford is "watching the clothes go round"—the boys sing this refrain in rapid repeat, like clothes tumbling dizzily in the dryer. There's a hint of race tumbling with the class consciousness too: "There go the whites, getting whiter; there go the colors, getting brighter." When she writes politically, Chrissie Hynde has tended to go straight for blunt attack or objection, but "Watching the Clothes" is sly, wry, and dry—one of her better protest songs.

Side one closes with "Show Me," an understated and under-rated song—one of her loveliest melodies. It's mostly a lullaby to her newborn daughter, but it's tinged with the same sociopolitical despair that colored "Back on the Chain Gang": "Welcome to the human race," she coos, but it's an apprehensive welcome: "with its war, disease and brutality." Her child has been born in bad times, which have given the singer "a heart of stone that's cold and gray." She hopes her baby can give her the break in the battle she sought in "Back on the Chain Gang": "Keep the despair at bay," she begs her infant, and "show me the meaning of the word"—love, of course.

Side two keeps its eye on the baby. "Thumbelina," probably inspired by Hans Christian Andersen's tale of the eponymous tiny girl and her adventures among the animals, invents a new genre, Lullabilly. "Hush little baby, don't you cry," the mother sings as they drive out west—to Tucson, oddly, where she had briefly lived during her return to the United States in 1975. It's the only cheerful song on *Learning to Crawl*, and the countryside they're driving through still has hillsides dotted with sheep, and rolling fields of wheat—the natural world that will have been paved over by the time "My City Was Gone" steamrolls in (it follows "Thumbelina"). "All the love in the world for you, girl" includes the verdant farmland. It's not until the final verse that the mood darkens, as it nearly always does in a Pretenders song. Mother and daughter are separated from Dad—you can't help picturing the man from "Time the Avenger," still staring listlessly out of his high office window with a drink in his hand—and they are not only on the road but on their own. "What's important in this life? Ask the man who lost his wife!" she fairly yelps at the very end.

Every Pretenders album contains at least one cover. "Thin Line between Love and Hate," an old Persuaders song from 1971, is a felicitous choice for purely euphonious reasons: *Persuaders* sounds a lot like *Pretenders*, and the verbs *persuade* and *pretend* have similar connotations. Both are about getting you to fall for their act. It's also a revealing choice for two reasons. First, along with the album's pointed references to Sam Cooke and Otis Redding, she delivers a clear message: *Learning to Crawl* may traffic in rock, purvey the familiar Pretenders Guitar Sound, and aim its music for the mainstream (that is, white) charts, but she's making a soul record. In a way, Chrissie Hynde always is; Jackie Wilson's kiss has never really left her lips. Second, whatever the status of her relationship with Ray Davies in 1983, when most of *Learning to Crawl* was recorded, it didn't elicit a cover of, say, "What a Wonderful World" or "Nothing Can Change This Love." The lyrics of "Thin Line" tell the grim story of another philandering husband, someone like the

Babbitt of "Time the Avenger," whose woman gets vengeance for his squandering of time: he has come home at five in the morning once too often and winds up "in the hospital, bandaged from foot to head." Even "the sweetest woman in the world could be the meanest woman in the world, if you make her that way."

"Thin Line" leads naturally into the slashing "I Hurt You" (but only because "you hurt me"), which sounds like one side of a complicated, resentful marital quarrel. "I've been wondering about your dependency," she sings, and "your idea of defiance." "Forget our philosophies," though; "we can't say 'I love you.'" She finishes him off with a prosaic putdown of his prosaic taste: "Never trust a user with your television overnight when the show he wants to video is *Dallas*."

The album's final song, "2000 Miles," is a sort of (please come home for) Christmas carol. The sweet tune, in lilting 6/8 time, was written in homage to Otis Redding's "Thousand Miles Away," and it also echoes the line "two thousand miles I roam" from his iconic "Dock of the Bay." Redding is the influence, but the song was deliberately and explicitly written for Jimmy Scott. "Sometimes in a dream you appear," she sings over guitars that chime the way Scott might have made them chime. Outside in the snow, "I hear people singing"—caroling, evidently—and what they're singing is a promise: "He'll be back at Christmastime." ("2000 Miles" readily lends itself to a strict Christian interpretation.) The song, still a staple of holiday season radio and one of her most covered tunes, closes *Learning to Crawl* on a complex note of both hope and heartache.

It's easy to imagine that the year 1983 closed the same way for her. Her daughter was a year old, there was a strong new Pretenders lineup—probably more accomplished (and certainly less inebriated) than the original one—and the US release of *Learning to Crawl* and a subsequent worldwide tour were imminent. She had enough brass in pocket to afford a nanny for Natalie while the band was on the road. But her relationship with Davies was frayed past repair, and both of them knew it. "The day before Chris embarked on her world tour in January of 1984, I carried Natalie into a church," Davies writes in *Americana*. "I said a prayer that basically asked for Natalie to be okay. I knew the separation was coming."[12]

Less than three weeks later, the Pretenders were in Melbourne, Australia, to play a couple of shows on their way to Honolulu. Then they were to enter America through its west coast backdoor and soldier through a prodigious eight-month tour of the continental United States in support of *Learning to Crawl*. She was licking her wounds, in deep grief over Ray.

Or was she? The Scottish band Simple Minds were staying in the same hotel. They'd played two shows at the Melbourne Sports and Entertainment Centre immediately before the Pretenders' shows. She met their singer, Jim Kerr, in the hotel elevator, according to a familiar story. Less than four months later they got married in New York. Ten months after that, their daughter was born.

Chrissie Hynde's romance with Jim Kerr is about as hard to understand as the one with Ray Davies is easy. Unlike Davies, Kerr had nothing musically in common with her. Simple Minds are remembered as an also-ran arena rock band, a sort of U2-lite who recorded the smash *Breakfast Club* soundtrack anthem "Don't You (Forget About Me)" and followed it up with the suspiciously similar "Alive and Kicking" and "Sanctify Yourself." ("Is that it for us?" Kerr later asked rhetorically about his band during an interview. "Rousing choruses and crashing drums?")[13] But in 1984, when she met Kerr, Simple Minds were a fey synthpop outfit with delusions of Depeche Mode, still in their baby fat of asymmetrical haircuts and *Cosmo*-girl makeup.

She could not have admired the way Simple Minds eventually broke through in 1985: it was with a song they didn't write, precisely the kind of musical cheat she had derided in interviews. ("A lot of these cunts, they take credit for stuff they haven't even written")[14] "Don't You (Forget About Me)" was initially offered to both Bryan Ferry and Billy Idol (the song was co-written by Idol's producer, Keith Forsey), then pressed upon Simple Minds by their label. Or perhaps, according to one source, "Don't You (Forget about Me)" was recommended to Jim Kerr by another singer who'd turned it down: Chrissie Hynde.[15]

Whatever the reason for the attraction, theirs was a hasty affair—for that is really what it was, six years of legal marriage notwithstanding. By midsummer, Simple Minds were opening for the Pretenders in America, and she was pregnant with Kerr's child for the remainder of her band's coast-to-coast tour, which was cut short when she reached her second trimester. She went back to the UK, swung by the studio where U2 was recording "Pride (In The Name of Love)," sang a background part—for which she was credited as "Mrs. Christine Kerr," presumably in order to avoid detection by Sire Records' legal department—and then headed right back to her house.

By the time the Pretenders' world tour ended in September 1984, half of *Learning to Crawl*'s songs had hit the American top twenty, and she was settled back in with her first daughter and awaiting the arrival of another with her new husband—whose band would break big in the US just a few months later with the release of *The Breakfast Club*. In the summer of 1985, Simple Minds and the Pretenders played consecutive sets at the landmark Live Aid show. It was the only date the Pretenders played all year. She was now the mother of two children; a rock star herself and married to one; responsible for a multiplatinum blockbuster album; and ironically, given the thematic plaints of *Learning to Crawl*, on top of both of her worlds, public and private.

But something happened on the way to the altar—of marriage and of rock and roll. Kerr went off to record Simple Minds' next album, and he never really came back. The Pretenders' next LP, *Get Close*, released near the end of 1986 when Natalie Hynde was less than four years old and her half-sister Yasmin Kerr wasn't yet two, included a scathing song about cad dads called "Chill Factor": "It's cold to leave a woman with a family on her own," she crooned, couching her fury in a sweet soul melody.

Although the couple didn't divorce until 1990, they were effectively finished years before, and Kerr remained largely estranged from his daughter until she was a teenager. The Great Pretender quickly hit the charts again but then became largely estranged from her music for nearly a decade.

FIVE

DON'T GET ME WRONG

Get Close and *Packed!*

How can she pursue her ambitions, be they great or small?"

—"CHILL FACTOR," 1986.

In 1985, with a platinum album and its string of charting singles behind her, Chrissie Hynde had the leverage to finance an even more mainstream move than *Learning to Crawl*. She returned to the studio without Chris Thomas, instead hiring Jimmy Iovine and Bob Clearmountain, two of the biggest producers going. The pair had (probably not coincidentally) produced the most recent Simple Minds album. She also traded up from drummer Martin Chambers, who was "playing crap," she said (one of her typically British locutions: not "like crap," just "crap"). "Martin just fucking lost it," she said. "And to think about it, why shouldn't he have lost it? He'd just lost his two best friends."[1] Elaborating on the choice to fire him from the Pretenders, she also revealed something about herself as both a musician and a human being: she wasn't as invulnerable as she liked to claim. "I was insane. I was traumatized. I was trying to keep my shit together. I knew musically I was losing my inspiration."[2] As she puts it in the lyrics to the first song on *Get Close*, "If there's a method to writing a song, how come I'm getting it wrong?" (And doing it less: she wrote only eight of the album's eleven songs.)

But she wasn't getting it entirely wrong. *Get Close*, which was released in November of 1986, yielded a pair of hit singles, went gold, and guaranteed her stock—which had increased in the meantime thanks to her 1985 cover version of Sonny and Cher's "I Got You Babe" with the reggae band UB40, whom the Pretenders had first heard in a London pub in 1980 and had promptly invited to open for them on tour.[3] "I Got You Babe" went to No. 1 in the UK and reached the top thirty in America. Yet *Get Close* also began the Pretenders' drift away from rock reliability and relevance, largely because it's a Pretenders album in name only, the first and most wayward of the hired-hand projects that sustained Chrissie Hynde's band and brand for the next twenty years—perhaps not dishonorably, but not quite coherently either.

The only real holdover from *Learning to Crawl* was guitarist Robbie McIntosh. He appears in photos on *Get Close*'s jacket and sleeve, along with drummer Blair Cunningham (recruited from Britpop band Haircut One Hundred), and bassist T. M. Stevens (formerly of James Brown's band). The new quartet was officially credited as the Pretenders, and they were the initial touring unit along with Funkadelic keyboard legend Bernie Worrell. But the album itself was recorded with a passel of session men and sitters-in. These included David Bowie sideman Carlos Alomar, who also toured with the Pretenders a bit and co-wrote one of the songs for *Get Close*, and Elvis Costello's bassist, Bruce Thomas. Even Simple Minds' drummer, Mel Gaynor, played on a few tracks. *Get Close* sometimes sounds like radio-ready pop; sometimes it sounds like funk; occasionally it even sounds like the Pretenders. But mostly it sounds like the times, and those times were the eighties. As Scott Miller wrote of that musical decade:

With eighties production . . . most of the world of feral and arcane studio sound obsession is simply gone in favor of a few simple rules, the first of which is that there has to be a big gated-reverb snare. And the mix has to leave plenty of room for this snare; there can't be too much guitar. This is like saying you can't hang a painting in a room with an 800-pound gorilla, because it will distract from the gorilla.[4]

Not five seconds into the first track on *Get Close*, "My Baby," there is the eighties snare—the entire eighties drum kit, in fact, big and echoing, along with the sterile digital keyboards, toothless guitars, and overprocessed vocals. "My Baby" even includes the cheesy sound effect of a crowd roaring, right after the self-doubting Pretender decides to "turn the page" of her despair over losing her songwriting touch by "walking on stage." The roar comes, significantly, from an unmistakably arena-sized crowd: she's famous now, and she knows she'll be performing this and other songs in large venues. Chrissie Hynde was hardly alone in this transition. Many bands, from Jefferson Starship to Heart, slicked themselves up for the eighties.

Every artist should be permitted the freedom to evolve, of course, to try new producers and sounds and styles and session players, but even the Great Pretender knew she had made an album that wasn't really the Pretenders, all the way down to the shoulder-padded blazer and bangle-sized hoop earrings she wore on its cover. The evidence of her dismay came shortly after the Pretenders began their 1987 tour. She quickly soured on the funk-flavored sound she was getting from her reconstituted band, although she could hardly have expected anything else from alums of James Brown and Funkadelic. If that sound had derived from some initial idea she may have had to make *Get Close* a funk record—which it was not, really—now she recognized the mistake.

At manager Dave Hill's urging, she fired Stevens and Worrell and replaced them with Rupert Black and Malcolm Foster, who had both been Pretenders on the *Learning to Crawl* tour. That reversion helped, but it couldn't salvage the songs on *Get Close*. There's nothing wrong with the jaunty "Don't Get Me Wrong" and "My Baby," both upbeat love songs of similar types, but the supporting material on *Get Close* palls. There's the vague eighties-aspirational therapyspeak of "When I Change My Life," a dart thrown at Washington politicians ("Dance!"), and another thrown at Pepsi-hawking Michael Jackson ("How Much Did You Get for Your Soul?"). The album also includes a surfeit of mushy romantic clichés and clumsy attempts to rework them: stars shimmering in the pools of your eyes, you'll always be a part of me, the sound of your voice like a lover's tongue, and so on. In solid eighties New Age form, and perhaps to bring her Hinduism to the public, she includes a few brief lines of Krishna chant at the end of "Tradition of Love."

Her taste in cover songs had devolved, as well. The rendition of Jimi Hendrix's "Room Full of Mirrors" is harmless enough, but the song Carlos Alomar wrote for her, "Light of the Moon," might be the worst one on the album. Her well-intentioned and competently delivered version of a song by a childhood friend from Akron, "Hymn to Her," reveals the saccharine sentiment at the heart of its feminist intentions. Perhaps the most sisterly thing about "Hymn to Her" is her longtime support of the song, which she was still featuring in live Pretenders sets as late as 2016.

Keeping "Hymn to Her" alive for her old friend was a typically practical and modest example of Chrissie Hynde's complicated brand of feminism. She has never embraced—indeed, has often loudly rejected—the role of feminist mouthpiece. She has gener-ally resisted feminists' attempts to claim her for the movement, and she has even gone after some of its sacred cows. She has never had anything good to say about the pill, for example. Her argu-ment that female birth control "misled" her generation has led her to conservative, even reactionary conclusions: not only her off-the-cuff line "a woman's gotta stay home some nights"[5] but also a dubious defense of her choice to have a child on the grounds that it isn't natural for a woman to keeping having sex without eventually accepting the procreative consequences. At the height of her fame she suspended, and nearly terminated, her career by dropping out of the public eye to be a stay-at-home mom for nearly a decade.

As a musician and bandleader, she is an unapologetic male chauvinist. She does not appear to have ever considered inviting another woman to join the Pretenders. "I didn't want it to get too emotional," she explained.[6] She almost completely rejected the "Women in Rock" phenomenon that burgeoned in the nineties—the skeptic in her probably spotted the marketing con behind it—and she has distanced herself from association with it throughout her career. Around the time of *Last of the Independents* (1994), when she earned her second-comeback veteran bona fides, she acted as an elder stateswoman only in a brusquely unsupportive, ten-point broadside called "Chrissie Hynde's Advice to Chick Rockers or 'How I Did It.'" It is printed on the insert for the CD single version of "Night in My Veins" and begins: "Don't moan about being a chick, refer to feminism, or complain about sexual discrimination." In No. 9, she rasps, "Shave your legs, for chrissakes!"[7] She added insult to injury by quickly disowning the advice (she claimed she wrote it facetiously at the behest of a music-biz colleague), leaving her adherents both scolded and abandoned. She finally gave Women in Rock her unofficial blessing by playing the Lilith Fair tour in 1999.

The opening track of the Pretenders' 1999 album *¡Viva El Amor!*, "Popstar," has only scorn for "your girlfriend": a pretender who "wants to beat the charts outta me. . . . She thinks it's so easy to get to the top." But in order to get there, she'll have to take her therapist's suggestion to "become a Buddhist" and "consider giving up red meat"—that is, try to imitate the inimitable Great Pretender, who tells the guy who ditched her for the pop star that he "should have just stuck with me." Later reflection did not soften her stance much. In *Reckless* some of her sharpest invective is aimed at Nancy Spungen, the doomed girlfriend of Sid Vicious; and her treatment of the Heavy Biker assault in Cleveland, as well as her refusal to back down from "tak[ing] full responsibility" for it, ran further afoul of the orthodoxy.

In her songs, however, especially the early ones, she elaborates

a very strong personal feminism derived from her lifelong experience of gender inequality, which includes a daily and vigilant
awareness of women's vulnerability to and oppression by men:
the sheer physical violability that is brutally exploited in "Tattooed Love Boys"; the disheartening, inexplicable tenderness
she feels for the guy who "hits me with his belt" in "977"; and the
dark but ineluctable craving for violent, anger-and-lust sex in
"Downtown (Akron)."

Like much of her worldview, her feminism is at once idiosyncratic, sophisticated, and materially oriented. It can be distilled
into a motto announced in a throwaway line at the end of "Lovers
of Today": "I'll never feel like a man in a man's world." The line
associates vulnerability and oppression with the greedy, competi-
tive, and antagonistic affairs of business: the prostitutes of "Kid"
and "I'm a Mother"; women as property in "Time the Avenger"
and as service personnel in "Watching the Clothes"; men off pursuing their dreams while women are left at home with the kids in
"Chill Factor." Her version of what theorists might call material-
ist feminism reacts to the dangers and consequences of inherent
physical imbalances and to entrenched systems of essentially
misogynist socioeconomic injustice, which can make a woman
a "jealous bitch, always wanting more," even though "the courts
have made her rich," as they have in _Pretenders II_'s "Jealous Dogs."
Money, power, and masculinity are intertwined. Often the only
way to survive as a woman in a male world—and the music business is one of its most sexist territories—is to look out for oneself.
That priority does not encourage much female solidarity.

Yet she'd felt that solidarity since college, if not before. A brief
moment in _Reckless_ not only shows that in clear detail, but also
functions as her feminist manifesto. It connects, in a single potent
image, the female body and child rearing, economic hardship, her
ecopolitical concern with cars and transportation, and the neces-
sity of going it alone in a foreign world, "man's" or otherwise. As
always, her feminism is entangled with the "endless war" that

harms not just women but animals, children, and the environment: it is an ecological feminism of sorts.

Near the end of her third semester at Kent State, not long after the shootings, she saw a poster nailed to a tree announcing a winter course in Mexico. In her typically impulsive way, she decided to sign up even though she had no need to learn Spanish—or any real desire to, if her subsequent delinquency is any indication. She cajoled the tuition out of her poor bewildered parents, who were by then so desperate to understand their rebellious musical offspring, which included her brother, that they'd resorted to taking a graphology class. But just as typically, upon arrival in Cholula, having tuned out Kent State's "chatterboxing females" on the bus, she took one look at the university compound surrounded by barbed wire and immediately looked for an escape. She found one hanging around, a dropout from Oregon who was checking out the new crop of girls. She invited herself to stay at his place away from the campus, where she barely set foot throughout the entire winter session. When it was over, she took buses around Mexico, seeking her vision of the "sandy beach" that reappeared, tantalizingly, in "Mystery Achievement" years later.

She did find the beach, but in the bus along the way she also found this:

> I was totally at ease sitting among farmers with their cages of chickens and sacks of grain and babies. I'd sit quietly at the back and copy the women with their arms folded tightly around their ribs to stop their tits getting trashed by the painful, violent jerking of bus over rock and gravel. Even with my flat chest it hurt like hell if I didn't hold tight. Those ladies knew. I was with people I had nothing in common with other than basic human elements like pain and hunger, but I felt, for the first time maybe, at home.

· · · · ·

If in the eighties, as Scott Miller wrote, "most of the world of feral and arcane studio sound obsession is simply gone in favor of a few simple rules," so too was Chrissie Hynde's feral, arcane—that is, treacherous and erratic—songwriting. *Get Close* offers none of the unorthodox time signatures, arresting chord and key changes, or other surprises that proliferated on the first three Pretenders albums. Her early departures from the traditional "method to writing a song" that she now fretted she was "getting wrong" on "My Baby" were the result of inexperience, not deliberate experimentation. Her songwriting intentions were never as radical as some of her compositions suggested, and she always preferred simplicity—the rock basics. She admired the economy of James Brown's ability to make a song out of a single chord.

She also liked it because she wasn't a good enough guitar player to do much more. "I couldn't really play along to records," she told an interviewer many years later. "I was alone in my room most of the time with my guitar, so I just had to write my own tunes so I had something to play." The 7/4 time and tritone changes she threw at early songs like "The Wait" and "The Phone Call" perhaps came from being alone in a room with no one to tell her those tricks weren't in the playbook. But she was a quick study: by 1980, Jimmy Scott could clue her in (rightly or wrongly) that B7 was a Beatles chord, and she could write a McCartneyesque pop song around it. But once she'd begun to master the method, her instincts abandoned her.

It was not only a matter of what had abandoned her, but also of what she had abandoned. *Learning to Crawl* made the Pretenders too big for her to keep writing and recording songs the way she had done before they were a mainstream act—and it's a shame. She would have been a perfect fit for the independent "college radio" that burgeoned beneath the top forty in the eighties, led by bands like R.E.M. and the Replacements: the alternative vanguard that generally relied on good honest guitars, lean, punchy production, and thrift store clothes. Many of these bands were almost as musically ideological as the punks she'd come up with in London, as strict in both sound and style. They were obliquely but consciously political too, especially R.E.M. With her rock head and punk heart, she'd likely have been very comfortable in the American underground. But there were two barricades. One was that college radio and its associated music were ethnically American, despite accepting some British immigrants, and by the mid-eighties she was ensconced in England with her family, an artist in two kinds of exile, geographic and domestic. The other, and larger, obstacle was made of platinum: as a million-selling rock star, she was no longer eligible for the musical margins, even had she wanted to join them.

Perhaps she didn't quite belong there either. Her pop instincts were too strong. "She has always seemed admirably comfortable with medium-level stardom," rock critic Robert Christgau wrote in 1999, not the cult milieu of the indies. Yet she was also "totally uninterested in iconicity of the Madonna sort,"[8] he added. She wasn't predisposed, temperamentally or circumstantially, to vie for one of the few spots for women at the top of the pops, which were mainly in the grip not only of Madonna (who had expressed admiration for her before becoming queen of the hill) but also of Whitney Houston, Janet Jackson, Cyndi Lauper, and a handful of others. She was not a manipulator or seller of her own image, and she still favored the same "masculine" style she'd started out wearing in the late seventies, which was anathema in the dolled-up, girls-just-wanna-have-fun eighties. Nor did she sound like herself under "the few simple rules" that controlled the musical moment. By the time she regained her bearings—it would take more than a decade—it was too late.

Still, *Get Close* yielded the No. 1 single "Don't Get Me Wrong." Whatever her fans think of this uncharacteristically cheerful love jingle, it has been a durable and crowd-pleasing staple of her live repertoire ever since: familiar, sunny, toe-tapping, and a welcome darkness-free song in any Pretenders show. All successful artists need songs like these, and her catalogue didn't quite have one until "Don't Get Me Wrong." She didn't care for "Brass in Pocket," whose midtempo beat and hard-to-understand lyrics make it hard to dance to and sing along with; "Back on the Chain Gang" is too melancholy despite its catchiness. The eighties may have gotten her wrong, but "Don't Get Me Wrong" did her right.

Plenty of eighties artists embraced (or were engineered or reengineered for) the decade's digital-driven music. The chintzy sound suited the eighties' driving musical force, MTV, which tooted everything through a television speaker and was far more about image than about music. The Pretenders were indisposed to buy into the rapidly expanding technology and production budgets of the music video industry, which had quickly dispensed with the amateurish cheek of early videos like "Brass in Pocket." These weren't the same Pretenders, anyway, and their only remaining original member hated making videos.[9] She was driven almost exclusively by creating music, not images, and she had an abiding reticence—even antagonism—toward the biz.

She also had two daughters to attend to, of course. At the height not only of her popularity but also of the most image-heavy decade in music history, she nearly disappeared from sight. The Pretenders barely toured in support of *Get Close* (some of the few dates were as U2's opening act), and she didn't play live again for an astonishing eight years. Her children, whose names were generally withheld from the press, didn't see her perform until they were in their teens. "Domesticity is the enemy," she writes in her memoirs. She once noted that Elvis Costello, who got started around the same time she did in London, had made forty albums; she has made only eleven.

It's no surprise that the strongest and truest message she puts across on *Get Close* is in the soul throwback "Chill Factor," which picks up where *Learning to Crawl*'s cover of "Thin Line between Love and Hate" left off. She explains exactly how you can make the meanest woman in the world out of the sweetest, while cagily borrowing the chords from another old soul song, "When a Man Loves a Woman" and undermining its devotional sentiment: "Your rise was due to somebody else's fall," she reminds Jim Kerr. She is not impressed on the children's behalf "whenever you make it home [and] shower them with presents." Although there's "resignation in her sighs," Chrissie Hynde has never given in to resignation, and she doesn't sigh for long. She barbs her disappointment with questions that issue both a veiled threat and a frank challenge as the song builds to its climax:

> She wants to be a good mother,
> She'll do the best she can.
> But what about the other?
> What about the man?

Although domesticity claimed her, she found occasional opportunities to visit the spotlight without making new music. A Pretenders singles compilation was released in 1987, and it remains the best-selling album in the band's UK catalog (it went triple-platinum there, gold in the US).

More important, she continued to sound her inimitable voice, not in song but in spoken word. She took her political vegetarianism on tour throughout the late eighties, lending support to Greenpeace and other organizations. Instead of kicking out Memphis police car windows, she used her boot on bigger institutional oppressors. At a Greenpeace rally in early June 1989, she was asked what she had done for the environmental cause, which had lately aimed its protests at the fast food industry's use of ozone-depleting CFCs in Styrofoam packaging. "I firebombed a McDonald's," she quipped.[10] Though untrue, the claim could be construed as an aspiration if not as an outright incitement. A McDonald's in England was bombed soon afterward. This was probably a coincidence, and no one was hurt, but accusatory eyes focused on her, and so did lawyers for McDonald's. On June 9, under threat of legal action, she issued a statement in cranky legalese: "I will at no time suggest or imply that I have been responsible for firebombing McDonald's or that anyone should firebomb or cause any other physical or personal damage to the customers, employers, franchises or the physical property of McDonald's Restaurants Ltd. or any of its associated companies anywhere in the world."[11]

Case closed, but her rancor toward McDonald's was just getting started, and CFCs weren't her only complaint. Twenty years later, in 2009, as a spokesperson for People for the Ethical Treatment of Animals (with which she has maintained a long-standing association), she staged a protest at a Salt Lake City McDonald's against the chain's inhumane slaughtering methods. "McDonald's means McCruelty as far as I'm concerned,"[12] she declared, wearing a red-and-yellow t-shirt with a creatively retouched McDonald's logo and the slogan "I'm hatin' it." Her image adorned a billboard that read, "Birds are scalded to death for McNuggets." She is as protective of animals as she is of children and has made provisions for her commitment to them to survive her: her will licenses unlimited use of her image and music to PETA after she dies.

Robbie McIntosh was invited to join Paul McCartney's band and left the Pretenders not long after *Get Close* came out. Needing a new guitarist for the Pretenders' late-1987 dates opening for U2, she recruited Johnny Marr of the Smiths. She'd mothered both Marr and Morrissey (a fellow outspoken vegetarian) through the Smiths' acrimonious breakup, although her sympathy for Marr's pain finally ran dry. "Two of my fucking band died,"[13] she told him; the Smiths were merely bickering over royalties.

Learning to Crawl had proven to her that the best way to get over the loss of a band was to keep making music, and soon enough she and Marr were attempting to co-write material for the next Pretenders album. The collaboration didn't last (there were rumors that the working relationship deteriorated when she habitually showed up stoned). It yielded only one song that saw the light of day, the blurry soft rock misfire "When Will I See You." She was left alone to write most of an album's worth of what she'd later dismiss as "stupid little pop songs."[14] That criticism is too harsh; song for song, *Packed!* (released in 1990) has fewer turkeys than *Get Close*, but it also has no "Don't Get Me Wrong" or "My Baby" (which also went to No. 1). The album doesn't suffer much from bad eighties sound, which was largely played out by the time *Packed!* was recorded; instead, it has virtually no sound at all. "Gimme a sense of purpose, a real sense of purpose," she sings on the lead single, as though quite aware that the album doesn't have one.

The album was produced by Mitchell Froom, whom she had probably met while both were contributing backup work to Elvis Costello's album *Spike*. Froom was a talented multi-instrumentalist, solo artist, and producer with a long and admirable resume that already included sessions with Bob Dylan and Paul McCartney. But the partnership was unsuccessful. Perhaps Froom misunderstood the nature of the songs she had written—or, more likely, she needed to have written better songs. Certainly she needed to be clearer about how she wanted them to sound. "I always knew what was right for the music," she writes in *Reckless*, but perhaps the music wasn't right for her, and she had no band left to help her figure it out. McIntosh was no longer around to husband Jimmy Scott's Pretenders Guitar Sound, and the fifth Pretender, Chris Thomas, was long gone. By the end of the eighties, she was the only one left, and even her presence seemed to be shrinking: the cover image of *Packed!* is a close-up but indistinct shot of only her eyes and bangs. Blair Cunningham, who played drums on much of *Get Close*, returned for the new album, but he wasn't credited as a member of the band. In fact, no band was credited at all. There were reports that she had put the Pretenders name on the album—in the band's original Art Deco font, perhaps for brand recall—only in order to fulfill a contractual obligation to her label, Sire Records.

Despite the lack of direction, *Packed!* is recognizably a Pretenders record—a muted one, but a Pretenders record nonetheless.

The lead track, "Never Do That," could have come from the same songwriting well that produced "Back on the Chain Gang" (the songs share a chord progression), and familiar face Billy Bremner—Jimmy Scott–approved and Nick Lowe–proofed—turns in a fine, Jimmy-style lead guitar performance. "Let me stay one more day," she begins, as though singing to the same lost soul she addresses in "Chain Gang," perhaps hoping to remain in that "place in the past we've been cast out of." *Packed!* marks the fuller emergence of a peculiar self-loathing streak that began to appear on *Get Close* ("Idiot me"; "I'm a peasant dressed as a princess"). "I don't deserve your time," she sings; then, on the second track, "Let's Make a Pact": "Cover me in dirt and leave me to the wind and rain." It's tempting to wonder whether she's borrowing from her Hindo-Buddhist worldview.

Her self-possession is never far away, however. Neither is her rancor. The galloping "Millionaires" turns her ire on fat cats and gets off a line of working-class irony: "We slash their tyres 'cause we're pathetic, and we get paid for the repairs by the millionaires!" (She makes sure to associate them with cars, her cardinal symbol of cultural evil.) This is a rather clumsy version of a fairly obvious idea, and the English pop band Tears for Fears had recently beaten her to it in their 1984 song "The Working Hour": "We are paid by those who live by our mistakes." Yet the way she yelps out that last word, "millionaires!"—in a country-rodeo half-yodel—gives the song a loopy and appealing energy; she makes you want to belong to the underclass her voice celebrates. She takes a certain glee in pulling a blue-collar fast one on the One Percent, and pride in knowing that "they'll never be like you and me." Whether a famous, well-off rock celebrity ought to be identifying with the proletariat is a more complicated question; but if Bruce Springsteen could take over the world that way with *Born in the U.S.A.*, why not the relatively unwealthy girl from Akron?

After "Millionaires" comes another Hendrix cover, although the only noteworthy feature of the bluesy "May This Be Love" is the bass—not the part itself, but who plays it: her old Jack Rabbit bandmate, Duane Verh. From there, the album settles into mostly uninterrupted MOR repose—music to listen to while you're making dinner for the kids.

Packed! ultimately fails by simple comparison. It lacks the attack, engagement, tension, and especially the risk of the Pretenders' best material. Even when it tightens its grip, it generally stays self-protective and sometimes even diffident. It's hard to imagine Chrissie Hynde, a decade earlier, asking her lover to "guarantee, when you're coming in me, you got a rubber on," as she does on "No Guarantee." Even after she boasts, "I'm potent, just one swig of me would get most guys smashed," she makes an out-of-character concession: "a drop of yours makes me stagger and swerve." The sacrifices of motherhood probably had more than a little to do with her reserved presence on *Packed!* But if her new modesty also led her to summon Froom, a producer with a well-established Adult Contemporary track record, it must be acknowledged that a songwriter's choice of producer is no less relevant to her conception of her music than her choice of guitarists (and clothes: "how you present yourself to your fellow man," she writes in *Reckless*). Froom seems to have toned down and tidied up everything she wrote—to have musically enacted the domestication that two children had required of her at home. His most effective rendering of any of the songs on *Packed!* is the laid-back reggae tune, "How Do I Miss You?"

Packed! is not a total dud, despite Chrissie Hynde's claims. The album is noteworthy for at least two songs. The punchy rocker "Downtown (Akron)"—the lone track from the album to be featured regularly in subsequent live Pretenders shows—is clearly a favorite of hers. It is both a paean to and a critique of her lost Akron, and at the same time an invitation to "downtown me": "strip me, chop me . . . bend me like a rubber dolly, demolition me," and finally "take me to the Cuyahoga Valley and make a man of me." You can do anything you like to her as long as it's in "the heart of the city" under "burning sulphur skies"—her awareness of environmental damage is always present—and as long as you use a condom: "Rubber glove me when you love me." This is a more prudent Chrissie Hynde.

"Downtown (Akron)" does two important things: it serves notice that she isn't through with "A, O, Ohio"—she'll still be singing about it almost twenty years later, on *Break Up the Concrete*—and it fuses the singer with the object of destruction: "demolition me, raze me, appraise me." When you destroy the city, you destroy her. Nonetheless, the singer is running right toward her destruction, going against the natural order. (As Love and Rockets sang just three years before, "Go against nature, it's part of nature too.") This is perhaps the essential dramatic tension in Chrissie Hynde's music. Although *Packed!* has little of that tension, "Downtown (Akron)" shows she still has it in her, musically as well as lyrically. The song is written in E, but the bridge purposefully moves through two other key centers, G and C, and then returns to E with her typically treacherous, erratic abruptness, yanking the ear around. At the end of the song she fuses two of the keys, landing on a G chord with an E in the bass.

The other song of note is "Hold a Candle to This," one of her few explicitly political protest songs that doesn't come off as merely shrill, bitter, or humorless (or all three). Her lyrical rhythm and rhyme are sharp and efficient, and her sense of humor makes a rare appearance: "So much for banning the bomb; the president's wife is carrying a hand gun" (a reference to a decade-old news item about the "tiny little" pistol Nancy Reagan kept in a bedside drawer). As the verses proceed, it becomes clear that the very title of the song is a sly act of political wordplay. When she exhorts us to "hold a candle to this," it isn't merely a call to light the way toward the coming "liberation." She wants us, especially the "farmer in the dell," to "blow up the abattoir! Detonate!" She may have withdrawn her vandalistic intentions toward McDonald's, but her ill will had not budged an inch.

The "liberation" doesn't end with the slaughterhouse. In the final verse of "Hold a Candle to This," she sings of the sailors who "mixed it on the shore; they were making love and making war." Lest they forget the girls they knocked up in "Osaka, Siam, and Saigon," she warns them that "those chicks will find you." The countries where the United States prosecuted wars are sending their women and mixed-race children to our shores to claim their American citizenship: "the new generation . . . same meat, different gravy." "Hold a Candle to This" is her funniest and loosest protest song, with a keenness and maturity not matched until the title track of *Break Up the Concrete* in 2008. It also happens to be the song on *Packed!* that sounds the most like vintage Pretenders—the two-chord strut of its verses recalls *Learning to Crawl*'s "Time the Avenger." She won't sound so much like herself again for nearly ten more years, or this at ease for ten more after that.

She had a very traditional, seventies-era conception of the rock franchise. First you got some singles on the radio, then you wrote more songs and put out a whole album of them, and then you supported the album by going on tour with your band. There again is her straightforward Midwestern pragmatism, married to her sense of the natural order. But the system fell apart with *Packed!* It yielded no singles of note. "Never Do That" briefly reached the top ten but was soon forgotten. The album barely cracked the top fifty in the United States, not least because the Pretenders (whoever exactly they were by then) did not tour in support of the album, even in England, because their leader was committed to staying at home with her daughters, who were seven and five years old when *Packed!* came out. By the early nineties, she discovered, to her dismay, "I'm not on the radio anymore!"[15] She had to make a decision about her future.

Many years later, she attended a wedding at which she was seated at the same table with Sarah Cracknell, the lead singer of the English pop band Saint Etienne. Cracknell would become one of the many women in rock influenced and empowered by the allegedly indifferent-to-Women-in-Rock woman rocker. "I was saying I hated touring and being away from my children," Cracknell recalled. "Chrissie was like, 'No, man, this is what you do, they're not gonna hate you for it.'"[16] In 1992, the Great Pretender took her own advice. She sat her daughters down and explained to them that although their mother was who she was, rock was what she did. That fall, she enrolled them in boarding school and set to work on the second comeback of her career.

"She has two completely different voices." © *Photo by Robert Matheu.*

Chrissie Hynde with the legendary photographer Kate Simon
in their early London days. Photograph by Joe Stevens.

James Honeyman-Scott, the inventor of the Pretenders Guitar Sound. © *Photo by Robert Matheu.*

Martin Chambers: after 1982, the only other "real" Pretender.
© Photo by Robert Matheu.

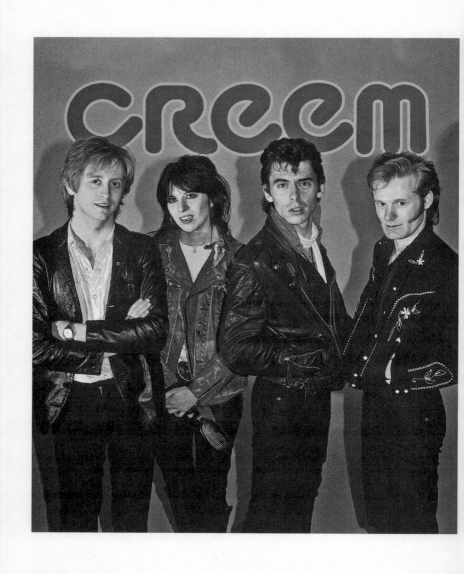

The Pretenders on the cover of Creem, *August 1980.*
© Photo by Robert Matheu.

On tour with the Pretenders, Detroit, 1980.
© Photo by Robert Matheu.

Chrissie Hynde with Ray Davies: "Ours was a battle of wills."
© Photo by Robert Matheu.

"The best part of Ohio": the Pretenders in Akron, 1981.
© Photo by Robert Matheu.

Chrissie Hynde getting hitched to Jim Kerr, before the chill factor set in. © *Photo by Robert Matheu.*

Detroit leavin': curtain call in the Motor City, 1984.
© Photo by Robert Matheu.

SIX

LEGALISE ME

Last of the Independents and *¡Viva El Amor!*

You should have just stuck with me.

—"POPSTAR"

If early in life Chrissie Hynde's nearest expression of a guiding principle was, "If I kept not doing what I didn't want to do, I would naturally get close to what I did want," then perhaps it was inevitable that she would eventually arrive here: "If you've been in the game a long time, the only things left that you haven't done are the things you never really wanted to do."[1] And so she did them, echoing the *Bhagavad Gita*: "The thing that, in your delusion, you wish not to do, you will do, even against your will."

Against her will or not, she decamped for Los Angeles, where, like a real rock star, she checked into the Chateau Marmont, Tinseltown's venerable celebrity address. She spent her days in the studio of songwriting duo Billy Steinberg and Tom Kelly, who specialized not only in writing hits, but in writing them specifically for women. The title of the first track on the ensuing Pretenders album, "Hollywood Perfume," was apt. You can smell its frank bid for mainstream success. You can also read it between the lines of the album's title, *Last of the Independents*, which attempts to declare the Pretenders as staunch anti-establishment resisters but, given its obviously commercial aims and alliances, is the most dependent album in the band's catalog. Almost all rock careers depend on hits, and she was on "a cold-blooded mission to get on the radio." She confessed: "I was ashamed of it, to be honest."[2]

That was why she enlisted Steinberg and Kelly. The duo had met in 1981 not long after each had contributed a song of his own to a Pat Benatar album. They started writing together, and in the early eighties they broke through with "Like a Virgin" for Madonna. They followed up that No. 1 smash with another, Cyndi Lauper's "True Colors," and proceeded to deliver a string of hits that included "So Emotional" for Whitney Houston, "Never" for Heart, and "Eternal Flame" for the Bangles.

Her collaboration with Steinberg and Kelly got her exactly what she wanted: a pair of top forty songs, "Night in My Veins" and "I'll Stand by You." The latter reached the top ten and has become an enduring torch anthem. Many singers have covered it, including Rod Stewart and Carrie Underwood, whose version reached the top ten in 2007. Chrissie Hynde may have been embarrassed by her own naked ambition, which included flashing some inner thigh and brandishing a guitar between her legs on the come-hither cover of *Last of the Independents*. (Liz Phair cribbed the shot and eroticized it even more for the cover of her eponymous 2003 album.) She was probably also embarrassed by "I'll Stand by You," a piano ballad that even Billy Steinberg worried was "a little soft, a little generic for the Pretenders."[3] (She rewrote Steinberg's most saccharine lines.) But Jeff Beck told her he liked the song, and Noel Gallagher of Oasis said he wished he'd written it himself.[4] Their praise, and the song's popularity, helped her come to terms with the Steinberg/Kelly upfit. She was on the radio again. The Pretenders were back, and back on the road.

Those Pretenders now included, once again, Martin Chambers, whom she invited to return to the drum kit. Although he played on just four of the thirteen songs on *Last of the Independents* (a pair of session players handled the other nine songs), he resumed full duties as the band's touring drummer, and his presence on tour betokened her priorities: she wanted the Pretenders to be a real rock band, and he was the only other "real" Pretender. (Chambers published his own memoir, *The Last Pretender*, in 2015.) She brought back Robbie McIntosh to play on one track of *Last of the Independents*, but the only constant in recording sessions was guitarist Adam Seymour, whose band the Katydids made a minor splash in the early nineties (their debut album was produced by none other than Nick Lowe). Seymour would stick around for a decade, playing, co-writing, recording, and touring as a Pretender for two more studio albums. He was the nearest replacement for Jimmy Scott that Chrissie Hynde ever found. Andy Hobson, who had already been on the band's margins—he briefly appears in the video for 1990's "Sense of Purpose"—played bass on three tracks and, like Seymour, stayed on for years. With them, the Pretenders achieved personnel stability into the 2000s.

Robert Christgau wrote a three-word review of *Last of the Independents*: "Style over substance."[5] It's a big, slick production, with something of the eighties sound still lingering. That is perhaps no surprise. It was produced by Ian Stanley, who made his name in the mid-eighties as a keyboardist and songwriting partner in the Britpop band Tears for Fears—what Simple Minds might have become if they had been forced to cover "Everybody Wants to Rule the World" or "Shout" (both of which Stanley co-wrote) instead of "Don't You (Forget About Me)." Stanley may have seemed a curious choice, but the studio makes strange bedfellows. She was aiming for the charts, and he knew how to get her there.

A different producer could have made *Last of the Independents* sound more like a vintage Pretenders album: her voice was still the main attraction, of course, and her songwriting sensibility hadn't changed much, Steinberg and Kelly notwithstanding. In fact, some of the lyric sets feel recycled from earlier albums, including the battered-woman psychodrama of "977." The song was apparently written in commemoration of her ugly breakup incident with Nick Kent in London's Sex boutique years earlier—so Kent claims in his memoir, *Apathy for the Devil*—but if so, it's an awkward joining of form and content: "977" is an oddly maudlin ballad. "He hit me with his belt," she gushes, as if Kent had given her a dozen roses rather than a permanent scar on her hand and a couple of STDs. And she succumbs to a depressing old trope: "When I saw my baby cry, I knew that he loved me." Even if that is meant ironically, it isn't convincing, not least because the song has no musical conviction: its musical sensibility doesn't match its lyrical content. It almost sounds as if Steinberg and Kelly had a prom-theme piano ballad already tracked and were waiting for a lyric set and vocals to affix to it. These happened to be the wrong ones.

"Money Talk," a punchy funk-rocker she wrote by herself, attempts to update "Kid": a prostitute negotiates business with a client in a car. But it concludes with the anything-for-a-quid mother complaining about fake breasts (which "won't feed the world like the ones that I pack naturally"). The most explicitly political song on *Last of the Independents*, the pointedly titled "Revolution," is musically nonrevolutionary soft rock. The song is a tribute to the Freedom Riders, hence her borrowing of the phrase "freedom will ring." It's the only instance in her songwriting career of explicit civil rights activism. Perhaps she'd been caught up in the documentary *Eyes on the Prize*, which repopularized the movement's history.

She may also have been inspired by her 1992 cover of Jon & Vangelis's "State of Independence"; she did guest vocals for a version of that song reworked by a duo called Moodswings, whose drummer, James Hood, played on a few tracks of *Last of the Independents*. The music video for "State of Independence" is laden with images of Dr. Martin Luther King Jr., and she appears among the masses crossing a bridge, freedom marchers-style. It's a nostalgic song, and so is "Revolution," which is why both fail to deliver any particular message. "Bring on the revolution," she sings, "I wanna die for something," although she never says what that something is. This too may be meant ironically—a critique, perhaps, of protest for its own sake, or even of the baby boomers' squandered ideals—but again the music lacks the bite to work as irony. The closest she comes to naming the fight is when she criticizes "the privileged classes" rather than institutional racism; her sensibility is always more naturally drawn to economic inequality (and, again, to children: "The children will understand why").

She stays politically engaged on "Every Mother's Son." The son in question "was born with my hand in a fist" and has gone on to use it to fight other people's wars. But the song that packs the most revolutionary punch is the far more personal and autobiographical "I'm a Mother"—perhaps coincidentally, the album's only song coproduced by the briefly returning fifth Pretender Chris Thomas. Over a funk-influenced track, she bellows her grievances to a world that has taken everything from her: milk, money, time. "I'm the source and the force you owe your life to . . . but to service mankind, I have to suffer his pride."

It hardly mattered that *Last of the Independents* contained mostly second-rate songs. An album needed only one big hit in order to sell well, and this one, like *Get Close*, had two. "I'll Stand by You" and "Night in My Veins" put the Pretenders back on the radio and back on the map. In 1994–1995 they toured internationally, now a tight rock outfit with Chambers behind the drum kit and Hobson and Seymour doing right by the spirit of Farndon and Scott. The Great Pretender was in fine shape—and, especially, voice, which could easily go unplugged.

A collaboration with the Duke String Quartet yielded the mellow and intimate live album *The Isle of View* (that's "I Love You" if you say it out loud), which, among other things, suggested that the expansive, complex "Lovers of Today" was, all along, a sonata in search of its chamber. They also made a big splash with their live recording, during the same session, of the Radiohead hit "Creep," all but reclaiming it from its originators: "I wish I was special," she sang, with a self-referential wink. Later in 1995 she appeared, bizarrely, as "Stephanie Schiffer" in an episode of the hugely popular American television sitcom *Friends*, stealing a singing gig at the coffee shop away from Phoebe (Lisa Kudrow) by entrancing the patrons with an acoustic version of "Angel of the Morning." "Stephanie" cheekily claims songwriting credit for the tune, which was actually written by Chip Taylor (who also wrote the Troggs' "Wild Thing") and made popular by Juice Newton in 1981.

That same year, she had a rousing homecoming when the Pretenders were invited to play at the Rock and Roll Hall of Fame Museum's dedication show in Cleveland just days before she turned forty-four. In her confrontational way, she chose "My City Was Gone" for her Ohio audience, to whom she gave town-by-town shout-outs before playing it. It was followed by a cover of Neil Young's "Needle and the Damage Done," essentially a eulogy for Pete Farndon more than a decade after his death. (The song would pop up in the band's live sets on future tours.) When the Pretenders themselves were inducted into the Hall of Fame a decade later, she called the institution "cheesy."[6]

Her star was at its brightest since the early eighties. In October 1995 she sang the National Anthem (badly) before a World Series game in Cleveland. As the year drew to a close, she made perhaps her boldest pass at the mainstream when the Pretenders cut the ribbon for another cheesy institution, the VH1 "Fashion Awards" show at the Lexington Theatre in New York. Uncharacteristically clad in a thigh-revealing miniskirt and wearing a bright red hair bow—and, most uncharacteristically of all, appearing without a guitar—she strutted around the stage, her band playing unseen behind her, and obliged the couture crowd with a strong performance of her nemesis song, "Brass in Pocket," boasting (as befits a fashion show) about using her style, arms, and legs. She pulled off the upscale burlesque convincingly, but then strapped on her guitar for a rocking "Night in My Veins."

Despite mastering the industry game, she evinced no desire to be strictly a pro. Kim Deal, who had made her name with the Pixies and then the Breeders (whose "Cannonball" had reached the top ten in 1993), was an avowed adorer—and a fellow Ohioan, having grown up in Dayton. In a 1995 interview with *Spin* magazine,[7] Deal recalled going to an Urge Overkill show—the band was riding the popular crest of grunge—at which her heroine, who had hooked up with the band, was called up on stage for a song. (In 1993, under the name Superfan, Chrissie Hynde and Urge Overkill had recorded a cover of the Carpenters' "Superstar" for the soundtrack of the movie *Wayne's World 2*.) "They did 'Precious,' and man, I was almost in tears," Deal said. "The whole muddy, ugly sound of Urge Over- kill just automatically cleared up. The sound system itself sounded better. She just did one song and it was so cool, so amazing."

After the show the band retired to a bar, where Deal spotted her idol drinking tequila straight from the bottle and making out with Urge Overkill's bassist. An introduction was arranged with the Great Pretender, who slurred, "You're not a chick, you're a dude." In an apparent attempt to seize the evidence of her claim, she "reached out and grabbed my boob. Then she grabbed my hand and put it on her boob, like it was a boob-off or something. I just got up and left. It was awful." Still, Deal concluded, "I'm kind of glad that she didn't turn out to be all nice and down-to-earth. She was kind of an asshole and I kind of liked that."

Going into 1996, then, Chrissie Hynde was back on top, and she wasn't about to abandon the route that got her there. She re-upped with Kelly and Steinberg to write more songs and came away with at least three, all of which were radio-ready and featured strong, sharp lyrics. They were better songs than "I'll Stand by You" and "Night in My Veins," and they recalled vintage Pretenders. Her band was on retainer. Her kids were still in boarding school.

But something happened on the way back to the airwaves.

It isn't clear what that was. Probably it was more than one thing. A major distraction was romantic: she met and fell for a Colombian sculptor fourteen years her junior named Lucho Brieva. We don't know how this affected her career—or much else about the relationship, of which we have even less evidence than we have of her involvements with Ray Davies and Jim Kerr. The very circumstances of her meeting Brieva remain a mystery. It is known that they were married in 1997, just six months after they met, in a half-hour "ceremony" at which she wore jeans to the registry office—as though she was finally living out the elopement dream she'd tried to realize years before, first with Sid Vicious and then with Ray Davies. The small wedding party, which included Annie Lennox, went out for cheap pizza and wine afterward. "We chose Pizza Express because it was so near to our home," the bride reportedly explained, deadpan.[8]

A planned 1996 Pretenders tour was postponed when she sustained a hand injury, apparently from a fan's overzealous handshake grip. (She still doesn't like to shake hands, and interviewers are instructed—warned, really—to greet her with a fist bump.) After that the narrative becomes unclear. In 1997 she appeared on the cover of *High Times* magazine, advocating marijuana legalization, and played at a concert in California held on National Medical Marijuana Day. Before launching into "Revolution," she made sure to "endorse the use of the herb for medical and other reasons. And I can tell you at forty-six that marijuana is the key to longevity."[9] In 1999 Robert Christgau reported that Lucho Brieva had apparently "cured her of a six-spliffs-a-night ganja habit."[10] That news—and her acknowledgment that "when I smoke pot, it can be demotivating, because if I'm not doing anything and I smoke a joint, it enhances just sitting in a chair"[11]—perhaps anticipates her much-later answer to a question about her songwriting habits: "It depends on how much pot I've been smoking, how many bottles of wine I've drunk." ("Time to kill another bottle of wine," from "Time the Avenger," could very well be a self-admonition, not just a criticism of the song's male protagonist.)

There is certainly more to it than drugs. Even with her children in boarding school, motherhood surely continued to pull some of her focus away from making music. But when she attributed the wide difference between Elvis Costello's forty-odd albums and her eleven to "domesticity . . . the enemy," she may have been withholding a deeper personal truth: she has simply never seemed driven the way Elvis Costello is. She works much more slowly, and "I goof off a lot more than Elvis Costello does," she admitted.[12] "My policy is to do the least amount to get by," she has said more than once.[13] Had she been a more ambitious and less principled artist, she almost certainly wouldn't have declined years' worth of opportunities to be in bands in London, Cleveland, and Paris in the mid-seventies before forming the Pretenders. She was apparently driven only by her stubborn mantra: "If I kept not doing what I didn't want to do, I would naturally get close to what I did want." Yet even when she got what she wanted and then diligently maintained the Pretenders for nearly thirty years, it was not in order to be prolific with them.

Perhaps she'd have made more music if Jimmy Scott had lived, or if she had not had children, but she has also explained her limited production in simpler and more straightforward terms: "I don't want to bore the public."[14] Her spirituality seems to be at work here: keeping to the "middle way"; doing neither too much nor too little; restricting the ego and its projections to their proper size. Perhaps she has always kept in mind Krishna's counsel to Arjuna in the *Bhagavad Gita*: "The whole world is a slave to its own activity." To her natural reluctance and self-restraint add the fatigue and injury of midlife (a word over which the word *crisis* hangs menacingly), self-medication and indulgence in whatever substances were available, and falling in love and marrying, and the setting, if not the cause, of a five-year gap between albums arises. It also seems likely that she was a victim of her advancing age in an art medium that prizes youth. Rock musicians nearing fifty can be hard enough to market; harder to market still are aging women rockers, who often suffer the full misogyny of the music business. She had twice rescued her imperiled career, once after the deaths of her bandmates and again after the births of her children. Whatever the cause or causes, between 1995 and 1999 her career foundered again.

More's the pity, because the Pretenders' next album, *¡Viva El Amor!*, was her true return to form, the band's best effort since *Learning to Crawl*. "The writing is sharp again," Christgau wrote. "The riffs have an edge, the lyrics bite."[15] It was produced by a pair of Stephens: Hague and Street. The former had been around for a long time, with production credits dating all the way back to a single he had produced for none other than Malcolm McLaren in 1984. Later he produced Siouxsie and the Banshees' biggest stateside seller, and he had worked with acts ranging from Pet Shop Boys to Blur to Pere Ubu (the latter an unlikely Ohio connection). Stephen Street had also produced Blur after making his name in the eighties as the Smiths' producer; perhaps Morrissey and Johnny Marr hooked her up with him.

The two producers brought plenty of experience and a sharp Britpop sensibility to the board, which in the late nineties was a great place to be. Recording methods had regained their footing, and the technology had substantially improved on the eighties' digital dependencies, which came to sound thin and primitive in retrospect. Punchy, hooky, Anglo pop-rock—exactly the kind the Pretenders once helped define—was having its day. The moment was right for *¡Viva El Amor!*

But *¡Viva El Amor!* was not the album Chrissie Hynde set out to make—not in name, anyway. She wanted to call it *Biker* in honor of the (Hell's) angel who had been on her shoulder and in her soul and guiding her songwriting all her musical life. But this biker was not the same tattooed love boy of her misspent early twenties, not "the beer-swilling rapist," as she described the Heavy Biker in a 1999 interview with *Newsday*.[16] If she had outgrown her destructive habits, so had he, at least in her rehabilitation of his image. Although the Biker rode the same machine and wore the same garb, he had transformed into a nobler version of himself: Che Guevara, who had taken his famous motorcycle journeys in another America, for a very different and much higher purpose, around the time she was born, and who appeared atavistically in the form of her new husband Lucho Brieva. He "kind of has a Che Guevara look to him," she gushed around the time ¡*Viva El Amor!* was released. (She showed a reporter a picture of Brieva pantsless, decorously covering his lower half with her hand.) Soon after they met, Lucho arrived at her front door in a biker's helmet. "I thought, 'Wow! It's him!'"[17] The "him" she meant was the New Biker: "an ideal: the renegade, the non-conformist who lives outside the law, with principles."[18]

"Cats like me and you adhere to laws outside the laws," she'd sung on "Revolution" five years earlier, anticipating the Biker's transformation. The Biker of her imagination had amended his ways, but he had not curbed his power over her. Another song on ¡*Viva El Amor!*, the hypnotic "Samurai," was written for "the ghost of a friend of mine," she said.[19] She could have meant someone as specific as Pete Farndon, but her lyrics give the samurai a spectral, spellbinding presence that strongly recalls the Biker: a killing machine, but a noble one, living by his own code, who still has her heart—and more: "When you came into my room last night and took off all your clothes," she asks rhetorically, "did you think I would resist?"

Warner Brothers would resist: They rejected her proposed album title, so she renamed it for what the Biker made her feel and added revolutionary language and imagery to it. She appears on the cover of ¡*Viva El Amor!*—alone again, for the fourth straight Pretenders album—raising a fist, Che-like, against a commie-red background over title lettering in Soviet-bloc font. The photo was taken by her friend and fellow-traveler on the vegetarian musician path, Linda McCartney. It was McCartney's last professional shoot; cancer claimed her soon afterward. Found in her darkroom was the developed image of the Great Pretender, who spoke at McCartney's memorial service in New York City.

The rejected title found its way onto the album in the form of a song by the same name. "Biker" isn't the raging rock number the title might suggest; instead, it's an elegiac torch ballad, complete with strings (the Duke Quartet returned from *The Isle of View*). "Biker, they tell me you're a dangerous lover," she sings. "That may be true, but I'd never ride with another." Her love for and devotion to the Biker, the "renegade with principles," has transcended cheap thrills and hair-raising encounters. Now, he is "an outlaw with a belief" who won't "conform to a godless society." He's religious, almost monkish.

Musically, the song is simple—it has only four chords—but ingeniously constructed. It begins in what sounds like E-major, rearranging a traditional I-♭VII-IV (E-D-A) progression to I-IV-♭VII (E-A-D), but the VII chord sits open, missing its middle note, as if waiting for a resolution. It isn't until the second verse, two minutes into the song, that an F#-minor chord appears, along with the string section, and on this chord the song deftly pivots into the key of A-major, its tonal center, which "Biker" has been masking with E-major until now. It's as though she is now fully revealing where her true allegiance lies, and how it lies there. The strings take the lead in an entirely instrumental bridge; there is nothing to say that the conversion to A-major, the real key, isn't saying clearly, even gently.

"You bring the biker out in me," she sings at the end of each verse, and that biker is as tender as violin strings. But at the end of the bridge, the song sits on E-major long enough to reestablish it as the key center, as though a dual consciousness persists. In the concluding verse she admires the way that "you, who have nothing, have something that only the One Percent could ever see." It's a curious inversion of logic: she predictably locates the Biker's true wealth outside "status and bogus desires"—that is, the spoils of materialism, which she has always protested—yet she identifies the audience for that deeper, nonmaterial wealth as the very same ruling class. They do still recognize the root value in the Biker's principles, which they may have abandoned for adult baubles but which still endure as the most stable and powerful currency of her generation. The high rollers of the booming nineties had been the hippies of the sixties. The song ends in an E-D-A circle, with the strings sweetly playing exit music for the entire album.

Although "Biker" comes last, it contains the organizing principle for ¡Viva El Amor!, and it isn't a stretch to imagine that it was intended as the album's lead track. It would be featured early in the set for Chrissie Hynde's solo-act Stockholm tour fifteen years later. But given its slow pace and anthemic mood, not especially suited to openers (and given her label's discontent with the very idea of the Biker), she put the tune at the end.

¡Viva El Amor! begins with the opposite of homage and praise, going after epigones and wannabes in a snappy, snarky song called "Popstar." We don't know whether its disdain is aimed explicitly at actress and model Patsy Kensit, Jim Kerr's latest flame, who tried unsuccessfully to launch a music career—or perhaps at Jim Kerr himself—but it certainly has something explicit to say to the countless indistinguishable music chicks and their handlers and fans, who all eventually start to "look like Kylie Minogue." In the video, arguably the Pretenders' best, Chrissie Hynde appears in an uncharacteristic but elegant black suit and lip syncs the lyrics while a parade of Spice and other Girls, including a Britney Spears lookalike, mug for the camera. (She must have been aware, though, that they weren't all pretenders. The nineties were the decade of Alanis Morissette, Liz Phair, Sheryl Crow, and other musicians of substance who had come to challenge her rule even as they owed her an often unacknowledged debt.)[20] The final chorus gives way to an ad-libbed, spoken-word dialogue with a venerable seventies punk, erstwhile New York Doll David Johansen. They sound like an old married couple, bantering (not entirely intelligibly) with each other about the chutzpah of kids today.

"Popstar" announces the Pretenders' renewed sense of musical focus and lyrical purpose, audible in a more successful second collaboration with Steinberg and Kelly—and there's an additional nod to them on the album's second track, "Human," which the duo didn't even write. "Human" was originally a Divinyls song co-written by professional hit maker Shelly Peiken, who also wrote the smash "Bitch" for Meredith Brooks. Divinyls' biggest hit was 1991's "I Touch Myself," which was co-written by Steinberg and Kelly. The Pretenders' cover of "Human" not only referred indirectly to her collaborators; more obviously, it gave a clever, punning nod to Divinyls' lead singer, Chrissy Amphlett, the second most famous Chrissy(ie) in rock. Amphlett, like Hynde, had been born Christine, had fronted a band of boys, and had developed a carefully cultivated look ("the schoolgirl" naughtied up); and like her forebear, she was notoriously mercurial and sometimes very combative.

The Pretenders' production of "Human" was not the first near-meeting of the two Christines; in fact, the choice to cover the song redressed a past conflict. Years earlier, both Divinyls and the Pretenders were on the bill of the 1984 Narara Music Festival in Australia, Divinyls' home country. Amphlett objected to the Pretenders' billing above Divinyls, who "should not be billed as second-rate," Amphlett complained. She refused to play the show. When the Pretenders took the stage, the older American was politic enough to call Amphlett her "sister in rock" and lamented that Divinyls weren't participating in the festival. Covering "Human" fifteen years later was another amicable (and atypically sisterly) gesture, as well as a mild act of self-defense: "I'm only human on the inside," she sings, not just a rival chick rocker; I, Chrissie, am like you, Chrissy.

A formal collaboration with Steinberg and Kelly, "From the Heart Down," follows "Human." It's another gushy tune, in the same prom-ballad mold as "977." But its refrain, "Love me from the heart down," conceals more than an invitation to bed. The lyrics speak to a midlife commitment to maturity and substance, in both the public and private spheres, that is evident throughout *¡Viva El Amor!* And the commitment isn't merely cerebral: the talk lovers share is just "analytical patter; you can't hold a theory," she sings. "The promise we keep" is to "watch each other even when we sleep, for some small protection"—that essential act of love, never far from her concerns.

Perhaps her marriage to Lucho Brieva elicited songs about adult love—which, with its nonconformist principles and strict codes of conduct and honor, is actually true love: true to itself, true to life, and also a refuge from life's mundane demands. "When the day comes to an end," she sings, "we take off all our clothes and stand naked, face to face with real life." "From the Heart Down" is a long way from the puppy love of "Don't Get Me Wrong," to say nothing of the sexual ordeal of "Up the Neck." And it's rare and encouraging to hear a nearly fifty-year-old woman rocker croon amorously about what mischief she'd like to make with her naked body, unwilling to relinquish its rights and privileges—and its desirability.

Another Steinberg-Kelly collaboration follows, "Nails in the Road," one of two pop-rock earworms that, unlike "Human" and "From the Heart Down," make no overtures to the radio and restore the Great Pretender's trademark toughness. "Nails in the Road" opens with the deft putdown, "If this is public transportation, what are you doing here?" The song aims its scorn at "royalty and people like thee," to whom the Ninety-Nine Percent can't get close even if they try. In the bridge, the song takes a funk break and departs from its F-major anchor, toggling between a C7-sharp-9 chord and a G-minor-7: messier sounds for a messier section of lyrics: "This is a cleanup job," she sings. "Everybody grab a mop." What they're cleaning up is "what floats on top," and by now she's savvy enough to omit the scatology. Instead, she reaches back for one of her treacherous, erratic changes. First the song goes up a half step, to A♭ major, and then to B♭, as though headed for a new key center at E♭, a whole step below the original F-major; but instead, the song makes a hard left, as though swerving around nails in the road, right from B♭ into G-major, a whole step above rather than below F-major. This is where a final verse traditionally ends up, higher than where the song began, but there is no natural setup for the change; she just crashes into it, driven by her predilection for abrupt transitions. It's a long way from the by-the-book key change of, say, Steinberg and Kelly's music for "I'll Stand by You," which makes sure to include a clunky IV and V before it makes its first big modulation.

The thematic and stylistic companion piece to "Nails in the Road" is the album's third and final Steinberg/Kelly collaboration, "Baby's Breath," another punchy rock song driven by Andy Hobson's cantering bass. The song is addressed to a haughty but childish, even prissy, ex-lover: "so pretty, so correct . . . in your designer jeans." (She seems to have an abiding hatred for designer jeans, one of her pet metonyms for poseur faux-rebelliousness.) The ex is not unlike the pop star of the lead track, callow but far from harmless: "You're such a child, but you're not innocent." Worse than lack of innocence, though, is lack of substance: save your roses "for someone's death; the love you have to offer is only baby's breath." You "thought you were magnificent," but even though "you're so pensive, . . . your thoughts are insignificant"— and she buries them with one of the most damning comparisons in her worldview: "Wrap 'em up, another twenty billion sold." McThoughts.

¡Viva El Amor! roams into some familiar territory. On "Who's Who," she scolds the selfish man from "Time the Avenger" and "Chill Factor": "Your future exists in her shopping lists. Please call your office." She regresses to her self-loathing tendencies in "Dragway 42," calling herself "lowly I." But as the album enters its richer, fuller second half, she also shows plenty of willingness to stretch herself and reach higher. Like an old R&B singer, she belts out some unexpected, show-stopping high notes, probably the highest of her recorded career, in the pleader "One More Time"— "Pleee-EEZE, won't you DO it one more time, DO it one more time, DO it one more time?"

In another nod to Lucho and Che, she covers "Rabo de Nube," delivering in Spanish a tender but deceptively tough-minded ballad by the protest-song troubadour Silvio Rodríguez—"the Cuban

John Lennon," as he has been called.[21] "Rabo de Nube" is a wish for a great cloud to come and, in a "downpour of vengeance" that is anything but gentle, wash away all the ugliness and sadness and leave an angel of hope.[22]

If the heart of ¡Viva El Amor! is in "Biker," then its mind is in "Legalise Me," which features a guitar cameo by none other than Chrissie Hynde's hero Jeff Beck. The rumbling, straight-ahead rocker, which borrows its basic two-chord verse structure from "Time the Avenger," approaches something like a Motorcycles with Guitars sound. It's a declaration of independence from all forms of tyranny, including the soma-like brainwashing of anti-depressants and the endorsement of violence inherent in the Second Amendment: "I don't take Prozac and I'll never own a gun." The song gives musical voice to her vaguely Orwellian (or perhaps Huxleyian) notion, which she's shared in interviews, that the pharmaceutical-industrial complex has co-opted the counterculture's recreational drugs by reengineering and repackaging them as prescription mood stabilizers.

Like any self-respecting sixties dropout, she's not just claiming her personal freedom but also "campaigning for the rights of the meek" while "holed up in a tree most of the week": political protest is bound up with personal retreat into the forest. The woman attacking institutional oppressors from McDonald's to the government also wants "the legal right to be me," both in the hollow of the tree and in full view of the world. "If I want to shake my hair in the sun, don't try to flail me for offending anyone." It's a total liberation of body, mind, and spirit, and of the people and their homegrown drugs. She boasts on the agrarian's behalf, "I'm just a farmer and I grow marijuana." She may have kicked her habit, but she hasn't kicked her principles.

And she reconfirms that she hasn't kicked musical invention either—that cardinally important "right to be me" as a composer. The song brings back the old Devil's Interval, the tritone from "The Phone Call," only to hopscotch back to its original key via an unlikely but ingenious series of chords. But then after the final verse, "Legalise Me" stays there on that Devil's Interval chord, using it as the new tonic for the song's rebellious, collapsing-into-shards finale.

The next song, "Samurai," is similarly complex. An arpeggio guitar figure lopes along over a squelchy drum track while the chords mostly go from A-minor to F-major, a fairly ordinary I-VI pattern. It's simple enough until the bridge, when it switches weirdly and with no transition at all into the key of C-minor, mainly relying on an unexpected half-step drop from E to E♭. The new key has virtually nothing in common with A-minor except the shared note of C. (She's fond of using that middle note as the new tonic, a nifty trick.) The same I-VI chord pattern ensues in C-minor until it substitutes an F-minor for A♭ major. This is a natural, rulebook-approved substitution on its own, but the F-minor chord winds up functioning as a turnaround back to A-minor, skipping the expected E7, a half-step below F-minor, that would help naturalize the modulation. Instead, she stays on F-minor and lets her voice climb up the scale from C, passing through a pair of notes, D and E, that are the main signals of the unplayed E7 chord and that imply the way back to A-minor. The whole transition, missing its crucial V chord, is strange and ghostly—as the samurai of the song is—yet to the ear it manages to sound nearly effortless.

¡Viva El Amor! got little publicity from Warner Brothers (they "just weren't interested in us anymore," she said), and it spawned a lone top forty single, "Human"—one of the two songs Chrissie Hynde didn't write. "Human" had also been included, slightly remixed, on the soundtrack to the movie Saving Grace, and that version was released as a single, with a video so sparse that it looks almost as if the crew packed up before the shoot and left her there alone with the camera. It's mostly a single close-up of her in a room that is nearly empty, save for a table and the chair where she sits lip-syncing. The only interference in this unadorned image is a pet dog, likely her own bulldog, Alfie, who appears at her feet midway through the song, the closest thing to a bandmate she has. "Human" reached No. 33 on the British charts and No. 30 in the United States, but ¡Viva El Amor! barely cracked the top two hundred, withering mostly unheard at No. 158. It was the last album she ever made for Warner Brothers. Her career as a bankable, mainstream rock star was over.

So was her marriage, soon enough. She and Lucho split in 2002. And another important man in her life departed as well, after a much longer visitation: Jimmy Scott. It seems his ghost had been not only lingering but advising her for years after his death; he was the good angel on her other shoulder. She writes in *Reckless*:

> I found that any musical questions I had could easily be an-
> swered. I just had to imagine what Jimmy would do. It was as
> if he was standing next to me talking to me. . . . That lasted
> another fifteen years or so, Jimmy in my ear, telling me what
> to do, and then slowly, he seemed to fade away.

If her math is accurate, that fade was complete by 1997 or so. At millennium's end, she was once again on her own, without her musical guide, a husband, or a record label. Her children were nearly grown. In 2001, she turned fifty. But she still wasn't done. She had more music to make, and it was music like she had never made before. She had more protest to sound, too, louder and more lawless than ever. She became what very few great artists become when the times lose their grip on them: a legend. And as a legend, the Great Pretender was at her most real.

SEVEN

COMPLEX PERSON

Loose Screw and *Break Up the Concrete*

> *Rely on my basic teaching:*
> *act always without attachment,*
> *surrendering your action's fruits.*

— *THE BHAGAVAD GITA*

She welcomed the new millennium by participating in a PETA-organized vandalizing of a Gap store in New York City on March 2, 2000, near the end of the Pretenders' tour in support of *¡Viva El Amor!* The Gap had unwisely attracted her attention by offering her $100,000 to use her recording of "Stop Your Sobbing" in their "Everybody in Leather" ad campaign. What she apparently intended as a simple, nonviolent attempt to champion the animal rights cause by getting arrested escalated after Gap employees tried to keep precisely that from happening. Probably fearing unwanted publicity, they refrained from calling the police on the high-profile activists, who also included PETA's president. To attract further attention, the protesters moved into a storefront window, where they held up signs depicting bloody cow corpses to shame the Gap for contracting with Indian leather goods manufacturers, who made their products in a country where cows were sacred and their slaughter largely (but not entirely) prohibited. Still no arrest, so they moved into the store proper and slashed up a few leather jackets. The Great Pretender spent a night in jail.

As though energized by her new freedoms, both artistic and

political, she quickly went back to work, co-writing songs for the next Pretenders album with Adam Seymour, whose tenure in the band was by then twice the length of Jimmy Scott's. Seymour had not only fully absorbed the Pretenders Guitar Sound; he had expanded it, giving it more polish than Scott had achieved but perhaps would have wanted, as a Beatles and Beach Boys devotee. She also rehired Billy Steinberg and Tom Kelly to co-write a couple of songs, and in 2001 she went back into the studio to record a new album. To produce it, she recruited another duo, Kevin Bacon and Jonathan Quarmby, who were best known for their co-production of a pair of 1997 reggae albums: the Brit Award–winning *Maverick A Strike* by Finley Quaye, and Ziggy Marley and the Melody Makers' *Fallen Is Babylon*, which took the reggae Grammy that same year. Her familiarity with at least one of her producers may have had an earlier source than those 1997 albums: Bacon's first band, the Comsat Angels, released their debut EP in 1979, the year the Pretenders were launched, and they had a brief semipopular run that lasted into the early eighties.

But it was the reggae she wanted them for. She'd thought of making a reggae album ever since her Ladbroke Grove days among the Rastafarians in the seventies, and *Loose Screw* (2002)—another apt double-entendre title, like *Learning to Crawl*—is about halfway there. It's part reggae, part Pretenders, with dub and other influences, all under Bacon and Quarmby's glossy, polished production. *Loose Screw* might be the Pretenders' best-sounding album, and it's their most sonically and instrumentally complex. It makes ample room for Andy Hobson's lush bass melodies; Martin Chambers's syncopated drumming, plus plenty of additional percussion; and unexpected but savvy use of keyboards, strings, and horns.

Yet in another way, perhaps befitting its throwback reggae model, *Loose Screw* is very traditional: it's a full-fledged relationship album in eight songs, from first flame to final flameout. The second track, "Time" ("Gimme some time, real good time"), leads to the fifth, the bump-and-grind soul number "Kinda Nice, I Like

It." Perhaps its "Everything about us looks wrong" is a reference to the wide age disparity and cultural difference between her and Lucho—"but it feels right," she decides. After that, things fall apart. First there's duplicity ("Lie to Me"), followed by separation ("Nothing Breaks Like a Heart"), regret ("I Should Of," with its curiously ungrammatical title—she clearly sings "I should have"), loss (the anti-anthem "The Losing"), an attempt at reconciliation ("Saving Grace"), and finally, in her time-honored way, one last kiss-off: the album-closer "Walk Like A Panther." This final track is a cover of a song by the band All Seeing I, co-written by Pulp's Jarvis Cocker, which only emphasizes how far she'll reach to put her message across. She borrows the song's lost Latino lover to stand in for Lucho: "Miguel has set up home, a woman half my age. A half-wit in a leotard stands on my stage."

It's unimportant whether the narrative arc is directly autobiographical. Whatever factual details the eight songs may contain are just that: merely factual, and secondary to another, less conspicuous but more coherent autobiography that lurks in the *Loose Screw*'s other four tracks. "Clean Up Woman" echoes "Watching the Clothes" from *Learning to Crawl* and "Chill Factor" from *Get Close*, depicting female economic subjection in the face of male privilege. "I'm here to clean up your mess," she announces, and that mess extends far from the laundromat and household, spilling out not just into the street but all the way into the theater of war. In "Middle of the Road" she impugned the "fat cats" who "own a big chunk of the bloody third world," and in "Every Mother's Son" she lamented the maternal rescue she'd have to provide for fallen soldiers. Her cleanup job includes not just "the mess he's made of the neighborhood" but "the kill of man's safaris"—her animal rights activism rearing up—along with "his battles of will," and finally "the wounds he sustains in his fight." So "she cradles him in her arms all night." Along with her resentment and her antiwar politics, the mothering instinct persists, in all walks of her own life.

In "You Know Who Your Friends Are," they're "the ones who want to see you go far," not the ones who hold you back. "Along by the canal"—surely one of the canals of London's so-called "Little Venice," just a stone's throw from her longtime home in the Maida Vale district—"you can see the remnants of last night's reverie" left behind by the partying locals: not "the gifts they give free in shopping malls," part of the familiar car-culture target of her ire, but "real life that's sprayed across the tunnel walls." This is graffiti, of course, a celebration of the same spirit of vandalism she brought with her into the Gap store in New York, but she once also mimed shooting up when she sang the line in concert. What's real is outside the law: the rule of the Biker, her beloved renegade with principles. "Loyalty," one of the Biker's strictest codes, "is just for those who've earned it," she sings later in the song, and then reprises a phrase from "Up the Neck": "You were hoping you could leave here with your teeth still in your head"; and the next line ends with the word "dead," another echo of "Up the Neck."

The song captures the suspicious mind of the rock star, who must stay on her guard against all the false friends, hangers-on, and backstabbers who haunt and harry celebrities. "I can't get from the cab to the curb without some little jerk on my back," she groused on "Middle of the Road" in 1983. Almost two decades later the jerks are still there; worse, it's harder to spot them because they come on like friends. You "tried to leave here for a working holiday," not for R&R, but because "your mother needed you two thousand miles away. But no sooner on the tarmac you were met to be told: 'We've been waiting for you; you just can't leave the fold'": the star-maker machinery can keep its stars out of the sky as readily as it can hang them there.

She goes after other enemies two songs later in "Fools Must Die," a driving, vintage Pretenders track featuring guitar work by Seymour that strongly recalls Jimmy Scott and Robbie McIntosh and cuts straight to the point: "The world rejoices when fools die," she sings in the first verse, then expatiates mercilessly on her schadenfreude all the way until the end, when she testifies to her own enlightenment: "Indulge yourself, as I have done. As you are now, so once was I." The message, stern as it may sound, is actually spiritual: we're all going to die, so we might as well try to live wisely and well until then and to achieve such contentment in ourselves as we can before the reckoning comes.

She was already preparing herself for that day at the end of the preceding song, "Complex Person," the album's central track: a self-portrait so blunt, prosaic, and honest—and so disarmingly reggae-mellow—that it almost sounds like a put-on. For most of its length, "Complex Person" sits on a single chord, F-sharp, with bare hints of a second. "I'm a very, very complex person," she announces, and then admits: "I try to improve but just see how I worsen." The confession turns into a warning, as her confessions often do: "I'll do anything to make you adore me—or deplore me—but never ignore me." From there, she rattles off a list of her flaws and predilections. "I've got senses that I cannae control"— they're still running amok as they were in "Up the Neck" nearly a quarter century earlier. Even past fifty, she's still a slave to her appetites and desires, an ever-androgynous "knave" who "can hardly behave."

And she's full of contradictions, too. "I'm a peacenik but I'm going off to war," although "I couldn't even tell you what I'm really fighting for" (an echo of her equivocal "I want to die for something" in "Revolution"). And although "it seems right," she finally throws up her hands and declaims, "I'm a mixed up, fucked up singer of a song." When she reaches the final verse of "Complex Person," she reiterates that she won't carry a gun (as she insisted on "Legalise Me"), but then asks us to

> Imagine if I was feeling perverse:
> The builders and the workers,
> When they whistle and they shout—
> I'd like to give them something to shout at me about.

The line is followed by a "whoo!" as if she's just scored a direct hit against her harassers—but as the song's title promises, it has a much more complex message and a much less combative character to deliver. Yet the message sounds at first like an afterthought. It appears in a line she sings during the fadeout, and it doesn't appear on the lyric sheet in the CD booklet: "I got a plan to give it all away. I won't need a suitcase on Judgment Day." She delivers the line just after the song has abruptly jumped up to a new key, A major, a jarring minor third above where it started. The jump grabs the ear—a complex key change for a complex person, and higher, too, for a higher consciousness—just in time for her to announce how she'll settle her contradictory life account of pluses and minuses. Yet it isn't actually an A-major chord that we hear, but an A-major with a suspended third, which leaves us with a sense of things unfinished, a balance still due, or a promise yet to be fulfilled. She's making a leap of faith in lyrics and music, and as always she trusts the ancient scriptural teachings of the *Bhagavad Gita*.

By the time *Loose Screw* was recorded she was beginning to allow her spirituality some public exposure. She wrote a short but enthusiastic preface for a book published in 2004 called *Holy Cow: The Hare Krishna Contribution to Vegetarianism*,[1] whose author includes this biographical note: "Chrissie Hynde's reputation as a singer-songwriter with the Pretenders has in recent years been eclipsed by her animal rights work. She visits India once a year to further her studies of Viashnava culture."

Leaving aside the dubious first claim—it's a stretch to argue that she has ever been better known (or worked harder) as an animal rights activist than as a rock musician—there are other points to interrogate here. For one, we have no documentation of Chrissie Hynde's visits to India. Where exactly she went, for how long, what she did, and with whom remains unknown to all but a few intimates. The fullness of her "complex person" has been revealed in her songs, and in her commitments to the Pretenders and her children and her activism, but seldom in her spiritual practice;

she works out her own salvation in private. Unlike one of her many epigones, Alanis Morissette, who used a well-publicized one-time "Goddess trip" to India to call attention to her spiritual quest, Chrissie Hynde practices her faith "alone in a room"—as she sings in "Up the Neck": quietly, over long years, under no scrutiny, and with no attachments. Her spiritual practice is not exclusively Hindu. "Boots of Chinese Plastic" from 2008's *Break Up the Concrete* begins with a phrase from a Buddhist chant, and when she referred in an interview to "the middle way" while explicating *Learning to Crawl*'s "Middle of the Road," she cited a Zen Buddhist text, the *Tao Te Ching*.[2] During the 2003 tour for *Loose Screw*, an interviewer found her hotel room strewn with religious books that included titles like *Teachings of the Christian Mystics* and *Rabbi Jesus*.[3] Nonetheless, the *Bhagavad Gita*, which she first discovered in her teens or early twenties, is the scripture with which she has "kept an ongoing relationship," she writes in *Reckless*: "the glory I bask in."

The *Bhagavad Gita*, which is part of the Hindu epic the *Mahabharata*, takes the form of a Socratic dialogue. On his way into a great battle, a warrior named Arjuna orders his charioteer to halt. He feels deeply conflicted, fretting aloud that killing is sinful. The charioteer reveals himself to be an incarnation of the god Krishna, and he exhorts Arjuna to fight: this is his work as a warrior, and if he does it in the yogic spirit, he is acting in good faith—provided he detaches himself from the results of his actions. (Hence, perhaps, "I'm a peacenik but I'm going off to war.") Krishna exhorts Arjuna over and over again to free himself from his attachments to earthly things—including the soldiers he must try to kill. They cannot be killed after all, for their spirits are immortal, encased in temporary bodies. (Perhaps this notion was a comfort to her and an inspiration to continue making music after the deaths of Farndon and Scott.) In order to practice this detachment, "You must first control your senses," Krishna commands, a message that surely hit home for a woman who found her "senses running amok" in

1979, and who in 2002 was still confessing, "I've got senses that I cannae control."

"The self is not the doer," Krishna tells Arjuna. Everything we do, and all we experience, including "the phone, the TV, and the news of the world" that are the source of so much pain in "Back on the Chain Gang," are nothing more than "sense-objects acting upon the senses." None of this is real: not a song, which is only a sense-object acting on the sense of hearing; nor a voice, which is made of air; nor the rock star it belongs to, whose fame is as notional and fleeting as a musical note. (Perhaps the name "Pretenders" has something to do with the *Bhagavad Gita*, even subconsciously, not merely her Biker's favorite Sam Cooke song.)

Krishna's most basic teaching is "act always without attachment, surrendering your action's fruits," which are neither real nor yours—mystery achievements. Her "plan to give it all away" in "Complex Person" will not merely be an act of soul-saving renunciation just before Judgment Day; she has practiced renunciation, or tried to, for most of her life. She turned her back on the materialistic, wasteful car culture of America; she gave up eating meat at an early age; and she has never been driven by money, or even shown much interest in it, leaving financial matters to accountants and managers. She doesn't even read her own contracts. She has generally lived as modestly as a celebrity can, even when she could afford not to. Her collection of designer boots is perhaps as much a necessary part of her rock star uniform as it is a personal indulgence. She has had some high-profile lovers and two marriages, but she has been romantically unattached for the vast majority of her life. In *Reckless* she writes that she has indulged in a few "dalliances, but for the most part have remained single. I enjoy my little meditations."

She does not pursue much public adoration either. Although she is beloved by her army of fans, she seldom courts their affection or even their attention. Her online presence, for example, is so negligible as to be functionally nonexistent. Yet while she may be a renunciate of sorts, she is "no recluse," as Robert Christgau observed.[4] She moves through the world in plain sight, seldom putting on airs, and isn't asecetic about her stardom. Danny Goldberg, who met her when his young indie startup record label, Artemis Records, bought and released *Loose Screw*, recalled: "She was very comfortable in her own skin; she liked being Chrissie Hynde."[5]

Goldberg was a veteran of the music business, and had briefly been the chair and CEO of Warner Brothers around the time of *Last of the Independents*, when the Pretenders were part of the Warner conglomerate. "It took me about five seconds" to make an offer when he heard *Loose Screw*, Goldberg said. "It had a fresh sound to it." (It contains a few inklings of the more European sound of her solo debut, *Stockholm*, released a dozen years later.) Artemis Records had been in business for only three years when Goldberg acquired *Loose Screw*—the Pretenders had made the album on their own and then opened it up to bidders—but the label had a commitment to signing established older acts who had run their mainstream course. When the Pretenders came on board, the Artemis roster already included Boston (another PETA-supporting act), Rickie Lee Jones, Graham Nash, Todd Rundgren, and Warren Zevon. The migration of big acts to small labels was a trend in the music business at the time. It not only relieved rock franchises of having to put up big sales numbers in their dotage; signing with indies gave them much more favorable legal rights and control over their own material.

Loose Screw sold even fewer copies than *¡Viva El Amor!*, topping out at No. 55 in the UK and No. 179 in America, where its quiet reception was no surprise to its publisher. "Although Chrissie is from the United States," Goldberg said of her, "she's fundamentally a British artist," and he knew the Pretenders' stateside appeal would be limited by her years of distance from the market, geographically, musically, and temperamentally. And she was about to drift even farther away, according to Goldberg, who recalled her telling him in 2002 that she was considering moving temporarily to Brazil. (She did so in 2004.) She had already spent time there during her involvement with Lucho Brieva, and Goldberg remembered her attraction to the idea of returning to a place "where she didn't speak the language, to get back in touch with her muse." The young dreamer who rode buses around Mexico in college was still seeking her sandy beach.

The Pretenders toured America for only six weeks to promote *Loose Screw*, although some of those shows were as the opening act for none other than the Rolling Stones. It was perhaps the perfect placement for the Pretenders at that juncture: right at the proscenium of the theater of the rock-and-roll gods, a familiar angel at the gates of music heaven. They were warmly received by Stones fans, who might have appreciated that the Pretenders' leader bore a more than passing resemblance, in dress and attitude, to Keith Richards—and she might have appreciated that her near-miss with Ron Wood decades earlier had finally arrived at a far greater consummation: she was sharing a stage with him, not a bed; she was a legendary rock star, not sleeping with one.

She was arrested again for protesting animal cruelty, in France in 2003. That same year, she extended her reach as a duettist, singing alongside partners as unlikely and varied as Gloria Estefan and Bruce Willis. Then she made good on her word to Danny Goldberg and moved to Brazil, where she met and worked with Moreno Veloso, son of the musical great Caetano. They toured with Adam Seymour, whom she brought over from England to play guitar. They did a lovely bossa nova version of "Don't Get Me Wrong" (an unexpectedly felicitous pairing of song and genre) and covered Caetano's "The Empty Boat." Working with Moreno Veloso was "one of the best musical things I've ever done," she said, "but for some reason, it was never documented."[6] She had moved into a hemisphere, geographically and musically, far beyond the Pretenders' territory, to a place where she was unseen and unheard.

Yet her legend was rising, and by the middle of the decade she had assumed her rightful role as one of the high priestesses of rock, joining the ranks of fellow Mother Courages such as Stevie Nicks (with whom she shared a manager, Gail Colson, having switched from Dave Hill). In 2005 the Pretenders were inducted into the Rock and Roll Hall of Fame. Her portion of the band's acceptance speech lasted thirty seconds, seven of which were reserved for a pause while the audience gave a memorial ovation to Pete Farndon and Jimmy Scott. Before turning the microphone over to Martin Chambers, she gave the audience her four-word, one-two punch of Zen-like, almost self-contradicting counsel, which she'd been heeding since childhood: "Boom boom: keep moving; never change." Yet in classic fashion, never quite willing to cede the spotlight, she jumped back in a couple of minutes later to add to Chambers's list of acknowledgments of some of the Pretenders' former members from the eighties. It took just seconds for their attempt at joint shtick to turn characteristically uncomfortable, with her repeating the "Martin was playing crap" line she'd first delivered twenty years earlier. He shoved her away from the microphone.

And then she came home.

She had unfinished business with Ohio, of course, but the real reason for her return was that her parents were getting older. She inverts the usual shape of stardom: she's the rare celebrity who has been unstintingly loyal to her family yet often unfaithful to the public, sometimes to the point of betraying the latter to honor the former. She'll put her career after her children, and her politics after her parents. In the eighties, the arch-conservative talk show host Rush Limbaugh started using the opening bars of "My City Was Gone" as his theme music. This was not because he approved of the song's politics (quite the opposite; he thought Chrissie Hynde was an "animal rights wacko") but because he liked Tony Butler's catchy bass line.[7] Word of Limbaugh's expropriation eventually got to her, but instead of ordering a cease-and-desist, she dismayed her fan base by allowing Limbaugh to continue using the song—for the unexpected reason that her parents liked his show. (She donates all the royalties to PETA.)

She sensed something happening in Akron, too, just as she'd smelled something in London in 1976. It wasn't as revolutionary as punk, but it was a sort of reclamation of youth culture: a revitalization of the Ohio of her childhood, which had long since been paved over by car culture. Her city was gone for years, but now it was coming back in the American urban renaissance of the 2000s. In 2008 she built a loft in Akron and opened an upscale vegan restaurant called VegiTerranean in the same building. At its opening ceremony, she rode down the street in an old-school diner outfit on the back of a Harley-Davidson, delivering a plate of food. That ride brought together two of the abiding archetypes of her life: Waitress and Biker. She began to split her time between London and Akron, where she took her political protest game to the field of public transportation, riding a city bus around town in support of a tax hike for the Akron metro system. That same year she played a concert with fellow Akronites Devo (a Sat Sun Mat fortieth reunion) and the Black Keys.

After *Loose Screw*, she thought the Pretenders might be finished, but they got more than a plaque at their 2005 Hall of Fame induction. There she met Steve Bing, a real-estate heir (and a playboy now better known for his paternity suits than anything else) who devoted some of his fortune to lefty philanthropy and entertainment ventures and dabbled in writing and directing in Hollywood. He wanted to start a music label and suggested a do-it-yourself Pretenders album. Two and a half years later, an entirely new Pretenders lineup made one for him: *Break Up the Concrete*. A photo of Bing carrying Chrissie Hynde in his arms like a rebel bride appeared in the CD booklet.

Martin Chambers told an interviewer that the incumbent band—he, Hobson, and Seymour—had actually recorded most of the album's songs in 2006.[8] If that's the case, their leader must not have been happy with the result, or perhaps Chrissie Hynde was just ready for a new sound. *Break Up the Concrete* is arguably the Pretenders album she might have made if she had never left Ohio or met the original Pretenders. She kept her bassist, Nick Wilkinson (who had already replaced Andy Hobson in the Pretenders' touring unit), but found a new guitarist—via Martin Chambers, as it happened. Chambers had discovered an English multi-instrumentalist wunderkind named James Walbourne, the secret weapon in the Pernice Brothers, an excellent American indie-pop combo. Walbourne would be her right-hand ax-man for the next seven years, capably assuming the role originated by Jimmy Scott and then held down by Adam Seymour. Wilkinson remained on hand for years, too. Bing helped procure legendary session drummer Jim Keltner, whom she'd met when the Pretenders opened for Neil Young, with whom Keltner had toured. But it was a fifth Pretender who signaled the Americana in the band's sound: not old friend Chris Thomas but a steel guitar master named Eric Heywood. The Pretenders were going to make a roots record—no, the Pretenders simply *made* a roots record almost as soon as they were assembled, before anyone had time to wonder when or how. It took less than two weeks.

Break Up the Concrete—another hortatory title in the Pretenders' catalog—was made in Hollywood in April 2008. It had no producer, other than "The Pretenders." It was recorded mostly live, with a handful of overdubs thrown on while she and Walbourne were waiting for the car to come and take them to the airport on the twelfth and final day in the studio. It contains audible throat clearings and missed notes, false starts and other mistakes, and even a long full-stop in the title track when Keltner isn't sure when to resume playing after the chorus. "Dak dak dak dak dakka-dakka-dakka-dakka" she counts off for him. Her great skill as a bandleader had only gotten stronger and more genially carried.

Perhaps her latter-day ease and confidence—no longer a bluff but the real item—are why *Break Up the Concrete*, despite its pickup-game feel and unedited bloopers, is the Pretenders' warmest and most organic album. It's a simple but supple collection of groove-based songs, some rockabilly, others jazz-inflected, still others R&B-driven, all unified by the quickly captured sound of the band and, of course, Chrissie Hynde's iconic voice.

The first track, "Boots of Chinese Plastic," is a crib of Dylan's "Boots of Spanish Leather," but first the album cribs an even older tune: *Concrete* opens with the famous slide guitar lick from Santo and Johnny's "Sleep Walk," then abruptly abandons it via her rapid-fire "one-two-three-four!," whereupon "Boots of Chinese Plastic" comes sprinting, very much awake, out of the gate. The song quickly discards its connection to its Dylan antecedent, keeping only a piece of the song's title. It has nothing to do with young lovers' mementos and everything to do with one of the priorities of age: philosophy.

She opens the song with a Buddhist chant, but by the end of it she has rolled Buddha up with Jesus and Allah, asking the latter for "a little mixed mercy." It's a song about reincarnation ("I spent a million lifetimes loving the same man"—the Biker?) and recirculation ("Every drop that runs through the vein always makes its way back to the heart again" is a rough translation of the chant that opens the song), but it ends with peaceable existential resignation: "Every dog that's lived his life on a chain knows what it's like waiting for nothing." He may not have his day, but in the meantime, she offers a small consolatory piece of flirtation: "By the way, you look fantastic in your boots of Chinese plastic." She doesn't intend this ironically: American rock's most famous animal rights activist hadn't bought leather for years. Chinese plastic may be a cheap, mass-produced, environmentally dubious sham substance, but it kills no animals; that's why you look fantastic in it.

Although she called the song "a protest of aesthetics," this lead track sets the tone for a late-life cessation (if not quite renunciation) of protest and an acceptance of contradiction, in which "heaven and hell ride in tandem" and we sagely choose the lesser of evils, plastic over animal cruelty. She is ready to reconcile with old enemies and with her musical roots, like Bob Dylan, and to get on the road toward grace. The concrete she wants to break up isn't only the ugly car-culture development she deplored from tour buses across America's endless miles of strip malls and freeway ramps; it's the hardened substance of old beliefs, attachments, mistakes, and resentments. Later in the album she wonders, "What kind of club opens its gates to sinners like me," who "spent my youth on a reckless futile race"? That song is called "The Last Ride," and the ride is with the Biker, whom she now considers neither a tattooed love boy nor Che Guevara nor a samurai. He's no longer a ruler of her passions or fears; he may still have his renegade principles, but to her he's simply "my buddy, my friend, my pal, my brother," and their ride is around Akron: "One more day to get it right," she sings, wistfully. To the degree that she can allow it, *Break Up the Concrete* is an album of letting go.

That doesn't mean she has entirely relinquished her thematic attachments. The second song, "The Nothing Maker," is another paean to the renegade with principles who "lives by a code known only to him"—partly because he's "a man who has nothing to show." He doesn't build anything, perform for audiences, or make art or even small talk: "You won't see him at parties." While other people "take more than they give," he doesn't even take abstract concepts: he "doesn't make money to buy watches and cars, 'cause there's no time and no place to go." With concise, elegantly aphoristic lines like this one, her generally prosaic lyrical tendencies finally emerge into a clearing of earned simplicity. The Nothing Maker is the Yogi Biker, and she still has faith in him—so "Don't Lose Faith in Me," she begs him in the title of the next track, an R&B come-on, even though "the artist on the cover is a phony and a crook. If you lose faith in me, you lose faith in us." In the fourth song, the rockabilly "Don't Cut Your Hair," she points back to Crosby, Stills, Nash, and Young while imploring her lover, "Oh, don't don't don't don't don't don't!" Yet it isn't just an homage to his hair. "They're all after the money, but you never got a taste for that." Keep the hair, renounce everything else: "That's why I love you, honey." Love and renunciation are bound up together yet again in "Almost Perfect": "Love is leaving everything for home-lessness and nothing."

But of course it isn't that simple; it never is with Chrissie Hynde. "Love's a Mystery" is the next song, a bright piece of folk-pop, and it starts with a wink: "Lovers of today," she sings, reaching back not to her influences' song titles but to her own, "aren't like lovers of the past," who "used to find a way to get a love affair to last." Not that she ever did, as she confesses: "I saw him leaving. That's all I had to see. If seeing is believing, then love's a mystery." Here again is the new economy of her prosody. Long a crammer of lines into meter, she now knows how to say more with less, as befits the sim-ple, stripped-down musical composition of *Break Up the Concrete*.

Along with her enduring subjects, she also retains her edge, her bad habits, and her spirit animal. "The Last Ride" begins with a dream in which she's "running like a horse" from "the man in red": shades of the recurring "demon" on *Pretenders*' "The Phone Call" and "Up the Neck." On the album's longest song, the odd, peripatetic "Almost Perfect," both her voice and the lead guitar snake chromatically up and down, giving the tune a tugging, druggy feel. She reclaims and rephrases an old, deeply sexist joke and delivers it cool and deadpan: "A lady who has two black eyes is not the best one to advise: she's already been told twice." Later in the song, she asks the "paranoiac, drug-addicted, pornographi-cally afflicted" man of her dreams—yet another whom she adores because he has no money—to "sleep with me: two legs, a cock, a woman's soul," And if that doesn't make her listeners uncom-fortable enough, in the final verse the fifty-seven-year-old drops in the phrase "oversized schlong"—which, by the end of the conclud-ing chorus, is "the best part of Ohio."

Ohio has other good parts on *Break Up the Concrete*, and she borrows them wholesale. The album's lone cover, "Rosalee," was written by Robert Kidney, who fronts the Ohio–based Numbers Band (as they're known; their actual name, 15 60 75, was deemed too hard for its fans to recall or repeat correctly). The Numbers

Band's members include her brother, Terry Hynde. "Rosalee" is the first panel of the album's final Ohio triptych. It's followed by the title track, a Bo Diddley–beat celebration and lamentation of her childhood street:

> There was a red brick road where I grew up on,
> And a pretty stone wall around a fragrant lawn,
> And fish in the pond that sparkled in the dawn,
> But it ain't no more it's all gone gone gone.

The chorus picks up the rapid-fire rhyming verbstorm she deployed on a much earlier song about Akron, 1990's "Downtown." Then, it was, "Chop me, adopt me . . . Raze me, appraise me."

This rhythm-rhyme style isn't limited to songs about Akron. She has long shown a fondness for it, as on "Legalise Me" ("Bail me, jail me, but they're never gonna nail me"), and it can be traced all the way back to *Pretenders*, in songs like "The Wait" and even "Brass in Pocket," with its fast, repetitive vocal phrasing and careful syncopation. Her melodic and vocal gifts aside, rhythm has always been her first priority. In "Break Up the Concrete," she gives the technique, and the city, a full working over:

> Ram it, cram it, grand slam it
> Prod it, sod it, metal rod it
> Whack it, thwack it, lineback it
> Shake it, bake it, earthquake it.

She finally comes to the conclusion that "we was so busy worrying 'bout them dropping the bomb," as she and most of America had done during *Learning to Crawl* and Reagan's Star Wars, that "we didn't notice where our enemy was really coming from": right inside the US of A. "Fat guys driving 'round in jeeps through the city" were actually in the city of Akron all along, putting in its "network of concrete and steel" and condemning it to its strip-mall demise.

Yet the song "Break Up the Concrete" isn't the LP *Break Up the Concrete*'s last word. The album ends with the slow, countrified "One Thing Never Changed," in which she is consoled that "that old train keeps blowing through the center of this town" even if the town has lost its heart (the heart her restaurant was trying to transfuse). "But it's gonna be alright," she sings, the essential lullaby line. She has taken the train home.

Break Up the Concrete was so modestly made that it wasn't even released as a stand-alone album outside the United States, but within the US a few corporate tie-ins with big-box chain stores like Walmart and Best Buy (hard to reconcile with her staunch anticorporatism) yielded multiple pressings with varying bonus tracks. In England no one offered her a deal, and *Break Up the Concrete* was released only as a "bonus disc" appended to a greatest hits package. The album cracked the top forty in the United States but remained there for just three weeks, and its singles faded about as quickly. She summoned Martin Chambers yet again and toured a bit—they played Farm Aid in the fall of 2008—but the concrete seemed finally broken up for good: the end of the road, and the end of the Pretenders.

There was no announcement of a breakup, no farewell tour, no elegies or lavish career assessments. Following best practices of impermanence and Zen, the Pretenders simply no longer were. Perhaps that goes a small part of the way toward explaining why it's difficult to say exactly *what* they have been over their three decades of life—to place the Pretenders in history. Other than Chrissie Hynde, the musicians changed, the sound changed, and the Pretenders' popularity changed. Thanks to her voice, they are always recognizable, but they are also uncategorizable, chimerical, as are their mixed Yankee-Brit origins. Their leader "personified the eloquence of sixties American pop and the nihilism of seventies England," Sasha Frere-Jones wrote in the *New Yorker*, getting at the Pretenders' initial roots in both pop and punk—yet leaving unsaid, perhaps appropriately, what the Pretenders conspicuously never were, despite the moment of their birth: a New Wave band.[9] They borrowed from many other genres but were always essentially sui generis (more and more so over their career as their sound continued to change), a bright but solitary satellite in the rock firmament. They did not spawn any clear direct descendants.

The Pretenders are the rare broadly popular and almost universally venerated act that has few if any imitators. Their songs are seldom covered. Chrissie Hynde's voice is inimitable, of course, but the Pretenders' inimitability is not limited to their recordings. The Pretenders are the only significant act of their time—perhaps of all time—made up entirely of men except for a female leader who has maintained total artistic control of the group from the beginning. The first time the Pretenders played together she regarded them as "my band." It is hard to name a single comparable group of any note in the history of rock. No other women have joined Chrissie Hynde on the trail she blazed, and even her own bandmates have not been entirely comfortable on that trail with her. In a 2009 interview, their oft-fired, always-rehired, grudgingly loyal drummer Martin Chambers called her "spoiled" because "it's all been her . . . and nothing else. And I think the whole Pretenders thing has suffered because of that." Such criticism has seldom been leveled at legions of rock frontmen who have wielded similar power and authority over their bands. Yet even Chambers acknowledged that Chrissie Hynde's vision was the indispensable essence of the band and that "part of his job in the Pretenders [was] to support Hynde in trying to make the best music possible."[10]

Even without the Pretenders, though, could there be more best music possible—or any music at all? There could, and there was.

EIGHT

YOU OR NO ONE

Fidelity!, *Stockholm*, and *Reckless*

True to the ethos of rock, Lemmy was forever unchanging.
It's one of those inexplicable phenomena inherent to rock stars,
the opposite of reinvention.

—*RECKLESS*

Perhaps Lemmy Kilmister hadn't changed, but despite the slogan
of Chrissie Hynde's Hall of Fame induction speech—"Boom boom:
keep moving; never change"—she has always been changing.
At twenty-one she turned herself English and changed her first
name. Then she was a Paris dropout, a Cleveland crazy, a London
punk, and an international Pretender. Her band's debut album
underwent multiple radical metamorphoses, from punk to pop to
balladry to soul, and the Pretenders transformed numerous times
over the years in both personnel and sound—sometimes by neces-
sity, sometimes by design, sometimes by her caprice. She went
from obscurity to celebrity; was half of a rock star couple, a sur-
vivor of rock tragedy, a comeback artist, a mother; half of another
rock star couple, a mother again, a single mom; then a has-been,
then a star again; an indie musician, a reggae musician, a roots
musician, a samba musician; an activist, a Hall of Famer, a has-
been again; half of a rock duo and finally a solo artist (as we shall
see). The ethos of rock, like the wheel, is always being reinvented
by its rockers; this is how they stay "Forever Young," the only Bob
Dylan song the Pretenders ever recorded.

If she looked older than her age when the Pretenders were getting started, she looked younger than her age when they gave signs of ending, little different in 2009 from the 1979 cover of *Pretenders*. She managed to stay the same by the paradoxical but necessary means of constant change. She liked the "Virgo qualities" in the clothes Vivienne Westwood made for Sex in the early seventies, so Chrissie Hynde might also appreciate this bit of astrology: around 2010 she arrived at her second Saturn return, which visits all of us as we reach the cusp of sixty. The first Saturn return, which occurs near the end of our twenties, asks us to commit to our occupation and the identity it will forge in us, as she did with the Pretenders in 1979. The second demands a reevaluation as Saturn's heavy, mortal energy leads us into the final phase of life. We take stock and try to make sage choices about what to do in the time we have left. We may make major changes, embark on difficult late work, or stake final claims. We may atone for old errors or revisit previous successes. We find that sensory pleasures and pains—what made our senses run amok—begin to subside in intensity. With a heavier but wiser head, tempered emotions, and steadier nerves, we enter life's dusk.

It isn't necessary to believe in astrology in order for it to rule us. (To reshape her Oscar Wilde borrowing in "Message of Love," we are all of us in the gutter, but all of us are ruled by the stars.) Whether Chrissie Hynde knew it or not, in her late fifties she began to follow the exact path of a second Saturn return. In 2008, at a bar, drunk—a familiar sense-object still acting on her senses—she met a youngish musician, also drunk, named John-Paul "JP" Jones (no relation to John Paul Jones of Led Zeppelin). History came with him. Jones was from Wales; Hereford, England, whence came the other three original Pretenders, is right near the Welsh border. The encounter with a handsome, younger, less-famous rocker was like meeting Jim Kerr in a Melbourne elevator a quarter century earlier. She and Jones fell for each other and went to Cuba, of all places: semi-licit and exilic, with echoes of Lucho Brieva and

Moreno Veloso, of "Rabo de Nube," perhaps even of Mexico's sandy beach and its mystery achievement. From a Havana hotel room she and Jones quickly wrote an album's worth of songs under the influence of rum, cigars, the first Moby Grape album, and each other: "We wrote to each other, about each other, with each other, and for each other," she said. Like her old flame, Ray Davies, she is one of the true romantics of our time.[1]

They went back to England and recorded the songs in November 2009 with some guys from a band Jones had played with, which he renamed the Fairground Boys because he had grown up working in an arcade around the fairgrounds his father owned and operated—and because he had wished his new musical partner "fairground luck" (a traditional Welsh parting) in a text message before a Pretenders show in 2008. She answered that he should write a song bearing that title. He did, almost immediately, and he sent it to her. True to form, she was leading the band before it was even there. In Havana they added another song, called "Your Fairground," which became the setting for *Fidelity!* It was not only another of her exclamatory album titles—like *Packed!* and *¡Viva El Amor!*—but also a triple entendre that touched on the sound of rock music, what the songs were about, and where they were written: high fidelity, romantic faithfulness, Fidel Castro. The album was credited to an act with the circus-like name of "JP, Chrissie, and the Fairground Boys." Roller coasters and carousels appear throughout the lyrics, distantly recalling the carousel in the Pretenders' video for "Kid" in 1981. But her fairground history went back much farther than that, of course. She'd been in thrall to the fair ever since Mitch Ryder and the Detroit Wheels' faux-fisticuffs at Chippewa Lake Park when she was a teenager. She associated the fair with "freedom and fun," she said.[2] Perhaps that old association made her feel like a kid again: falling in love, running off to Cuba, and making music. But behind the arcade and the tent, the fairground is in shadows; Saturn's darkness—the darkness of age and coming death—is always encroaching. The wry, melancholy joke and deeply mortal theme of their gritty but well-made roots-rock concept album is that she's too old for JP Jones.

Whether they ever consummated their passion or not is unimportant; they made it clear that they never actually became what we'd consider a couple because it was simply impossible. "I found my perfect lover, but he's only half my age," she sings in her half of the album-opening duet "Perfect Lover": "He was learning how to stand when I was wearing my first wedding band." She's prepared for him to leave her and marry a younger woman who can bear him children, but "meanwhile, I'll be the one," she assures him. Later he sings, "I couldn't blame a man to leave a woman past her prime." That sounds cruel and chauvinist—but she's the one who wrote the line. She liked his delivery of it so much that, ever the bandleader, she insisted he take the lead vocal on that part of the song. She liked everything about him, it seems. "He's the best singer-songwriter I've met."[3] Ray Davies's ex and Paul McCartney's friend must have been very drunk on love to make such a ludicrous claim.

In 2010, JP, Chrissie, and one of the Fairground Boys performed a twenty-minute, late-afternoon acoustic set at Lollapalooza. Little girls pranced at the lip of the stage. She sat before a microphone and sang and cracked jokes and played the tambourine, looking genuinely relaxed, content, even confident. Lollapalooza was the highest-profile gig of her new band's American tour of small clubs, where one or two hundred people might show up. She didn't seem to care about this downsizing. It had probably been since Jack Rabbit in 1975 that she'd had the luxury of playing in places like these, a world away from the arena. She had never craved fame, only a band, and now she had the best of both worlds: the freedom, status, and inspiration to play exactly the music she wanted; and the detachment from its material consequences to play it exactly where she wanted. She did not need to make money, hit records, or news. She was just making music. She loved JP Jones's voice and songs (and him), and she was determined to use her living-legend leverage to get the world to hear them.

It didn't work. (Neither did her restaurant VegiTerranean. It folded in 2011, trailed by lawsuits.) They had released *Fidelity!* on their own record label, La Mina (another double-entendre if you read it backward), but their artistic autonomy left them little promotional support. Although the album was generally well received by critics, it got no publicity to speak of, failed to sell, and didn't make JP Jones a star. The duo made no further music together, and within five years even their band's website was defunct. (So is the website of Jones's subsequent solo project, *Son of Jack*. He has since mostly retreated to the studio as a professional songwriter for hire.)

The Fairground project had little material consequence for her, but it may have enabled the true second-Saturn moment of Chrissie Hynde's career. She had never been anything but the leader of the Pretenders. Now, having finally played without them, she was ready to keep exploring. Yet there was no apparent portent, no band feud or crisis of identity or self-image of the kind that befell David Bowie at Ziggy Stardust and the Spiders from Mars' final gig. She was guided by her steady, sturdy Midwestern pragmatism and work ethic, that canny sensibility that could even get her to think like a businesswoman at times: "It's a way of rebooting my brand," she explained, when she was asked why she took down the Pretenders' shingle and hung out her own.[4] It's hard to imagine her younger self thinking of her brand—or to imagine her sixty-three-year-old self thinking of rebooting: she is a confirmed technophobe who describes herself as "a digital immigrant."[5] And she had always insisted on having a band, even if it had to be frequently reassembled—her three-decade maintenance of the Pretenders only amplified her principled commitment to rock as a group endeavor. It's also awkward to hear one of her songs ("I'll Stand by You") licensed for a Progressive Insurance ad,[6] and more awkward to see the name "Chrissie Hynde" on the marquee of a venue called Bojangles' Coliseum, named for that fast-food bastion of sausage and fried chicken. But perhaps Saturn's second return was repeating her own mantra back to her: "The only things left that you haven't done are the things you never really wanted to do."

So out came *Stockholm*.

It certainly didn't sound like a Pretenders album, but most of *Loose Screw* and *Break Up the Concrete* hadn't sounded like Pretenders albums, either. Perhaps *Stockholm* proved once and for all that it hadn't been clear for many years exactly what constituted a Pretenders album, other than its frontwoman on the cover. There she was alone again on the cover of *Stockholm*, but the word *Pretenders* was absent, replaced by *Chrissie Hynde*.

The album has echoes of her past, of course. "Dark Sunglasses" picks up on her tradition of snarly, snarky album openers, from "Precious" to "Popstar," but it's actually the second song on *Stockholm*, following the softest, most vulnerable leadoff track of her career: the reverential, yearning, lonely-hearted "You or No One": "Love is a hurting thing. It doesn't go away." Her initial tone has changed, although her politics have not: the song's video is PETA propaganda. And although "Dark Sunglasses" goes after another poseur pop star, this time it isn't a rival chick rocker but a guy she may have played with in the past (JP Jones, perhaps?). He has given up the sleeping-in-the-van life for a pension plan and church on Sundays. There's something almost poignant in the way he hides now behind his dark sunglasses, and something trenchant and weighty in the essential truth that she leaves unsaid because the song itself says it for her as it plays: she's still rocking, and "she'll be rocking till she drops," as Neil Young promised when he inducted the Pretenders into the Hall of Fame.

Stockholm has a tune that she called "The Neil Young Song" before she wrote lyrics for it, because it sounded like one to her. So after it was finished, recorded, and renamed "Down the Wrong Way," she got Neil Young to add a guitar part to it, as she'd had Jeff Beck do on "Legalise Me." (She also got her old pal John McEnroe to play guitar on another of *Stockholm*'s tracks, mainly to wow her tennis-buff producer, who got to hit a few balls with the aging bad boy of the court.) The lyrics to "Down the Wrong Way" contain a reference to a fairground and the words "misty valley." Her album with JP and the Fairground Boys contains a song called "Misty Valleys." "Down the Wrong Way" also includes the line "You made her an offer that she can't refuse." All of this seems to bear out the prediction on *Fidelity!* that Jones would "leave a woman past her prime" for someone younger, but it would be a mistake to insist on a strictly autobiographical interpretation, as it would be to pin her to the song's opening line: "I've become what I criticized." Everyone does eventually, she explained when asked about the line, adding that she borrowed it from ancient Hindu scripture— not the *Bhagavad Gita* ("The thing that, in your delusion, you wish not to do, you will do") but the even older *Vedas*. To further deflect an autobiographical reading of the song, the longtime cinephile noted that another of its lines came from the Harvey Keitel movie *Bad Lieutenant*.[7]

Chrissie Hynde's lyrics, like most rock lyrics, are best taken as figments and fragments of a "mixed up, fucked up" imagination that gathers and arranges the pieces and sets them to meter and rhyme—not always comfortably, concise in neither sound nor sense. A lyric's intention can change radically by the time it is sung, and most of the work is discarded anyway: "Take this page and throw it away," she sings on *Stockholm*'s last song, "Adding the Blue": "Fill the holes in, sand the wall," as if she's made a final decision to erase the whole album, all the way down to the spot where it hung while she made it.

One thing is sure: don't take her at her word, not even her last word, because she has seldom thought her words through. The lyrics to "Adding the Blue" were written in twenty minutes (she raced to complete her verses for the Pretenders' early recording sessions in the seventies, too). It's a song about painting, which she had taken up in later life. Or perhaps she had always been a painter. She'd gone to art school all those years ago, although she insists that "I'm not Monet or Van Gogh" (not even close: "I can't draw like S. Clay Wilson," she sings, referring to a cult cartoon-ist, one of R. Crumb's primary influences). Although "this was gonna be my masterpiece, the paint's not even dry yet" when her model gets up and leaves midsession, absconding with her inten-tions and designs "while I'm adding the blue": the color, perhaps; the feeling, certainly. Art, Da Vinci said, is never finished, only abandoned, and sometimes it isn't the artist but the subject who abandons it. The artist may continue to paint around the place where the subject had been, "trace the outline of a shadow," and try to remember what she set out to paint in the first place. On the cover of *Stockholm*, Chrissie Hynde wears her classic togs—vest, no shirt, low-knotted tie, tight jeans—but her face is warpainted Swedish blue and yellow. She is both artist and canvas.

The album is called *Stockholm* because it was recorded there in bits and pieces over the course of months, produced by a pair of Swedish collaborators recommended by her publisher. No double entendre title this time; no politics to peddle, no point to make; no specific stories to tell and few scores to settle. *Stockholm* has no songs about Akron or animals, babies or bikers or the bomb. There are scarcely any personal details at all. They've been stripped away save for a brief reference in "House of Cards" to her brother Terry during an alternate-verse, spoken-word child's prayer (an ill-advised moment, frankly). The song called "Tourniquet (Cynthia Ann)" is so oblique and personally addressed that the Cynthia Ann in question remains a phantom, haunted by eerie *The Good, the Bad and the Ugly* whistling.

She said she no longer had the need to write lyrics grounded in specificity, despite what songs like "Down the Wrong Way" and "Dark Sunglasses" may have vaguely implied about JP Jones, and she'd earned the right to draw from the collective rock lyric well: the great generic tradition that summons "every cliché in poetry" (as she sings on "You're the One"), in which *baby* automatically rhymes with *maybe* and you can't judge a book by its cover. Yet *Stockholm* isn't clichéd at all. It has a light but steady hand with extended metaphor and parallel construction, and a sage brevity that suggests more than it says. The ordinary line, the simple and direct thought, is where she's at her best. "Feels like the universe just grew." "You left here with nothing but something to hide." "A big blue sky and a plan too far." And then there is "Don't fuck with this heart of mine"—another strong word against airplay, sung right after the isolated phrase, "good pretending." The Great Pretender is still at it, after all. *Never change*, and despite her nominal brand reboot she hasn't, not even under the Swedes' Eurodance beats and techno textures, which are pleasantly inflected by Wild West effects, tumbleweeds rolling across her late-career music.

She hasn't even altered her essential methods. Although *Stockholm* is a solo record, she repeatedly insisted that it was even more collaborative than most Pretenders albums. All eleven songs were co-written with her producers, Björn Yttling and Joakim Åhlund (there are no covers). The chord changes are generally simple, nothing treacherous or erratic, the instrumentation often interesting but always unobtrusive. The only notable compositional departure is a fondness for nonguitar keys, especially early in the album, like E♭, B♭, D-minor, and G-minor. (Later, there is a curiously unbroken run of four straight songs in the more familiar key of E-minor.) Perhaps the songs were composed on keyboard rather than guitar, or transposed to accommodate her voice, which had dropped into a lower register over her years of smoking cigarettes. She was virtually a tenor by now, and reduced to a narrow range, yet her voice remained as toned, rich, and singular as the day the Pretenders were born. And as natural: some of her vocals on *Stockholm* are the original demo tracks she laid down during early recording sessions. She rebooted the brand, not the operating system.

The release of *Stockholm* was naturally followed by the customary tour, mostly in smallish concert halls. The band's entrance music was Sam Cooke's version of "The Great Pretender." (The exit music was Morrissey.) She started off with surprises: "Don't

Lose Faith in Me," "Biker," and "977": lesser-known, mid- and late-period Pretenders songs most of the crowd probably hadn't heard. The rest of the show mixed selections from *Stockholm* with better known Pretenders songs, but she sent a clear message by conspicuously omitting "Brass in Pocket." Limping visibly from years of knee problems or perhaps a fresher injury, she nonetheless rock-starred her way through shows with latter-day Pretenders James Walbourne and Nick Wilkinson, but without Martin Chambers. Her voice, at sixty-three, sounded as if it had scarcely aged a day; and the rebooted brand brought back Chrissie Hynde's old customers, to whom she preached between songs: "Old is good. Would you really want to do all that again? Fuck that." Then she gave them a little Zen 101: "Anyway, this is all temporary. Let it go."

There was only one thing left for her to let go: her secrets.

Now that her parents had passed away, she finally felt liberated to write the memoir she'd been considering for a decade. She started jotting down vignettes until they began to cohere. *Reckless* was published the day after her sixty-fourth birthday in 2015. The subtitle is *My Life as a Pretender*, even though 80 percent of the book takes place before the Pretenders existed, from her infancy to 1979. Her publisher probably wanted the word "pretender" in the title to remind the uncertain shopper of the author's identity, but perhaps the reason for its inclusion goes deeper than that: "Pretender" isn't merely a job title or a band, it's how she has lived, playing the character and wearing the eyeliner of Chrissie Hynde. The story she narrates, like her confidence, is a bluff, and all of life's achievements are mysteries.

Unlike many memoirs, *Reckless* has few hatchets to bury or axes to grind. It contains very little dishing or bashing, except of its narrator, whom she scolds for many misbehaviors, especially rampant drug use (which is perhaps why she sharply criticizes Nancy Spungen, who took Sid Vicious down with her—the cardinal sin, in Chrissie Hynde's worldview, of harming the vulnerable). She protects both her real family and her rock family, assiduously concealing the most intimate and potentially damaging details. She almost entirely skips over her romance with Pete Farndon, never making their relationship seem personal but giving him some business for his drug addiction. She says virtually nothing about Martin Chambers, who has been her most enduring musical confrère. Malcolm McLaren comes off as a visionary prince, Jimmy Scott as a flatulent angel. Though it may have been true, as John Lydon said, that Vivienne Westwood called her "a despicable little piece of shit," she does not return Westwood's fire and instead writes of her admiringly. She doesn't even slag lawyers or record company execs, the safest targets in the world (Morrissey whines on and on about them in his *Autobiography*). And she wishes "an onward and upward journey" to a Heavy Biker she took up with for a while; she has "a soft spot for him, wherever he is now (he's dead)."

Reckless is tight-lipped in the years it omits as well. The book's chronological account ends in 1983, before her split with Ray Davies, who gets scarcely a page of attention, mostly in the form of her comical recounting of one of their rows. Her children do not appear, and Jim Kerr never makes his entrance; nor does she make her own into the arena of political activism, save for a few references to car culture and brown rice. The days and demands of motherhood as a rock star, something readers might like to learn about, are left entirely untouched. If, as she writes, "domesticity is the enemy" of writing songs, in her view it's surely also the enemy of writing memoirs, She must have known that the part of her life with the broadest appeal, and that stretched across the broadest canvas, spanned from her arrival in England to the deaths of Farndon and Scott, and these years make up the bulk of the book. But she is also protecting her children, as always. *Reckless* is dedicated to them, but it is not about them. The memoir manages to be at once brutally honest and carefully guarded, just like its author. Much of it recounts familiar stories and opinions, at times nearly verbatim from other sources; thus the chronicle has the feeling of well-traveled territory, thoroughly but predictably revisited.

Critical response to *Reckless* was lukewarm. The book might have made only a small ripple in the flood of rocker autobiographies drenching the market in the new millennium had she not stirred up controversy after it was published. She's always had "a mouth that flapped like a rag tied to a post in a windstorm," she writes in the lead-up to her account of the Heavy Biker assault in Cleveland—an account that attracted quite a bit of attention from readers and critics, almost all of it negative. Making her promotional rounds for the book, she was repeatedly asked whether she really thought she should "take full responsibility" for the attack, as she claimed in *Reckless*. She stood by her words—and perhaps, symbolically, by her man, too: the Biker, that powerful and complex force in her life who gave her not only some of her deepest wounds but also the clearest vision of her band, some of its best songs, and its name too. To the media, she reiterated the book's insistence that "you can't fuck around with people, especially people who wear 'I Heart Rape' and 'On Your Knees' badges." Getting out of her mind on Quaaludes and willingly going home with a bunch of Hell's Angels was asking for trouble. "No one dragged me into the bushes with a gun to my head," she said, and further stymied interrogation by adding, "I never said I was raped."[8] The book's description of the attack elides nearly all of the details, rendering the scene mostly in fragmentary dialogue. She alludes to something awful but avoids actually describing it.

She could not, however, avoid the consequences, which came at an unusually sensitive point on the timeline of women in rock. Jackie Fuchs, known as Jackie Fox when she was a teenager in the all-female rock band the Runaways, had recently revealed that Runaways manager Kim Fowley had drugged and raped her. Meanwhile, Grace Jones had taken her private life public in a memoir of her own, and had devoted a chapter to trashing upstarts like Miley Cyrus (much as Chrissie Hynde had done in "Popstar"), whom she felt had ripped off her style, lacked true identity and vision, and would have no staying power. The issues of female agency, vulnerability, and solidarity in the rock world were quite charged at the moment *Reckless* was published, and the general dismay and disillusionment turned toward its author. The court of public opinion charged her with "victim blaming," and she absorbed harsh, widespread scolding—which, ironically, amounted to still more victim blaming. Jackie Fuchs weighed in disapprovingly. Lucinda Williams, whose career and persona owe the Great Pretender some little debt, took to Facebook and spat, profanely, as her forebear might have if similarly irked, "I can't believe this fucking shit! Come on, Chrissie!"[9]

Near the end of her month-long promotional gauntlet, the embattled author appeared on *Morning Edition* at a National Public Radio affiliate in Minneapolis.[10] "Chrissie Hynde is a tough interview," the host, David Greene, avowed (or warned) in an introduction recorded later. Her responses to his initial questions were terse and tense. In the version of the interview that aired, her answers are heavily edited and often interrupted by Greene's ex post facto contextual elaborations, so it is hard not to wonder whether he had somehow antagonized her before the interview even started. She objected that he seemed to be asking her merely to repeat what she had already written in *Reckless*. The book, like her music, spoke for itself. "The rest of me isn't really up for grabs," she said, a tidy reiteration of an abiding personal rule. Toward the end of the interview, Greene asked her about the Heavy Biker assault and her unyielding public comments about the "responsibility" she took for it in the memoir. He reminded her that she had told the *Sunday Times of London*, "If I'm walking around in my underwear and I'm drunk, who else's fault can it be?" Probably quite weary of responding to charges of victim blaming, she went on the offensive:

HYNDE: So what are you getting at? Why are you asking me this?
GREENE: I just think a lot of people—

HYNDE: I don't understand why there's—you know what, I don't care what a lot of people want. You know? I'd rather say: Just don't buy the fucking book, then, if I've offended someone. Don't listen to my records. 'Cause I'm only telling you my story, I'm not here trying to advise anyone or tell anyone what to do or tell anyone what to think, and I'm not here as a spokesperson for anyone. I'm just telling my story.

ACKNOWLEDGMENTS

I'm first and foremost indebted to American Music Series editor David Menconi, who invited me to write a book. Without him, *Chrissie Hynde: A Musical Biography* wouldn't exist. I also owe thanks to editor Casey Kittrell, whose counsel throughout helped me clarify my thinking about my subject—a persona who at times can be anything but clear— and to the peer reviewers and copy editors who helped me improve the manuscript. I'm also grateful to Larry Butler, an éminence grise of the music business, for his correspondence; and to Danny Goldberg, the founder of Artemis records, for taking time to talk to me about *Loose Screw* and his association with the Pretenders and Chrissie Hynde in the early 2000s.

Jim Henderson has been my musical mentor since I was a teenager, and I returned to him for another set of ears to help me hear the complexities in Chrissie Hynde's music. Some of the musical analysis in this book would not have been possible without him.

Scott Miller was the frontman of the wonderful but neglected pop bands Game Theory and the Loud Family. He is also the author of a remarkable book of music criticism, *Music: What Happened?* It's an extraordinary survey of more than fifty years of pop and rock, and a de facto autobiography. In it he singles out "Up the Neck" as his favorite track from *Pretenders*, a characteristically obscure but trenchant pick by an obscure but trenchant artist. Miller's choice prompted me to revisit the song and discover in it a hidden source of Chrissie Hynde's worldview, storytelling power, and emotional depth. Except for chatting with him for a few minutes after a Loud Family show in 1996, I never knew Miller, and sadly I'll never have the chance. He took his own life in 2013, just fifty-three years old. Game Theory's albums have been posthumously reissued, but Miller never got his due in life. For every Chrissie Hynde who manages to make her name and career through her music, there are surely countless Scott Millers who never do. May this paragraph go some small way toward keeping his memory and music alive.

When I was a teenager, my father bought me my first keyboard and helped me build a custom case for it. On the day I graduated from high school, my mother wrote to me, "I hope you will always feed your roots with music." Here, finally, is the first fruit. I thank my parents for their investment, love, care, and patience.

This book is dedicated to my wife, Heather Mallory, and she has earned more than the dedication (and half the royalties). She is also the source of this book's subject. One night in 2014, she and I sat up in bed volleying ideas, and she was the first one of us to say "Chrissie Hynde." I can't come up with the right words to thank her, so I'll borrow the Great Pretender's: *I said baby, ah, sweetheart.*

SOURCES AND NOTES

The most frequently consulted sources for this book are Chrissie Hynde's recordings, from *Pretenders* through *Stockholm*. Whenever I found myself seeking clues, personal details, thematic and character development, or even simple inspiration, I went to her music first and most often. Music seldom lies, and when it does, it seldom gets away with it. The written word can be more slippery. What artists say about their work and lives is notoriously unreliable. For that reason, although Chrissie Hynde's memoir *Reckless* (Doubleday, 2015) provides more evidence than any other text in this biography, it's by no means authoritative. In many cases, even the stories in *Reckless* that seem clear and concise simply repeat what she has been telling interviewers for years. See, for comparison, the interview transcriptions in Jon Savage's invaluable history of punk, *England's Dreaming* (New York: St. Martin's Griffin, 2002), and its unabridged companion, *The England's Dreaming Tapes* (Minneapolis: University of Minnesota Press, 2010). Her reiterations of these accounts complicate rather than clarify the picture because the stories we repeat about ourselves are often strongly skewed, retouched, or carefully curated for the record. When Chrissie Hynde said of Martin Chambers in 1987, "Martin was playing crap," and then said it again in 2005, she may or may not have been telling us the technical truth; but she was certainly telling herself what she needed to believe when she fired him, and perhaps what she needed to believe when she fired him again two decades later.

Fortunately, much of Chrissie Hynde's own account of her formative years in London can be checked against others'—a reasonably satisfying sketch of her life and character from 1974 to 1979 could be drawn from memoirs by contemporaries like Viv Albertine (*Clothes, Clothes, Clothes. Music, Music, Music. Boys, Boys, Boys*, Thomas Dunne, 2014), Nick Kent (*Apathy for the Devil*, Da Capo Press, 2010), and Johnny Rotten (*Rotten: No Irish, No Blacks, No Dogs*, Picador, 2008). A deeper dive into interviews and other sources, most of them online, reveal more nuance. Wherever possible, I've compared most of the details Chrissie Hynde divulges in *Reckless* to their presentation elsewhere by other participants.

Two essential sources for the Pretenders' early days are Kurt Loder's 1980 *Rolling Stone* profile of the band ("The Pretenders Ain't Sobbing," *Rolling Stone* 319, May 29, 1980), which includes many quotes, and James Henke's subsequent *Rolling Stone* profile of Hynde from 1984 ("Chrissie Hynde Without Tears," *Rolling Stone* 420, April 29, 1984). Scott Cohen's 1986 *Spin* profile ("Hynde Sight," *Spin* 21, December 1986) helps complete the narrative of the original Pretenders lineup, from 1979 to the deaths of Jimmy Scott and Pete Farndon in 1982 and 1983, respectively, along with what little we know of Chrissie Hynde's relationship with Ray Davies, whose *Americana* (Sterling, 2013) provides additional details.

A good deal of Chrissie Hynde's public life has been lived during the internet era, and although she is sometimes prickly toward the press, she has given many interviews over the years and can even be quite voluble under the right circumstances. The most useful interviews, for my purposes, were "The Blue Railroad Interview" with Paul Zollo (bluerailroad.wordpress.com/chrissie-hynde-the-bluerailroad-interview), itself an expansion of an interview Zollo did with her for *American Songwriter* (http://americansongwriter.com/2010/12/chrissie-hynde-the-great-pretender); Oliver Hall's lengthy *Arthur Magazine* interview with her and late-model Pretenders guitarist James Walbourne in 2008 (http://arthurmag.com/2008/12/17/pretenders-qa); and Marc Maron's 2014 WTF podcast interview (http://www.wtfpod.com/podcast/episodes/episode_556_-_chrissie_hynde). She does not put on airs or try to throw interviewers off the scent. She's both outspoken and plainspoken, she's consistent in her beliefs to the point of dogmatism, and she says exactly what she thinks. It's for this reason that she has sometimes spoken controversially, even perhaps when she didn't intend to. She is sometimes a victim of her own directness, with "a mouth that flapped like a rag tied to a post in a windstorm," as she puts it in *Reckless*. When she says nothing, or nearly nothing—about her romantic relationships and her children, for example—this reveals perhaps as much about her as anything she has left on the record. The music and lyrics she has left on the records—nine (now ten) studio albums with the Pretenders, and a solo album—fill in nearly every missing detail for the willing ear.

· · · · ·

INTRODUCTION

1. Larry Butler, personal correspondence with author, October 2015.
2. "Chrissie Hynde: I'm Just Telling My Story," an interview with NPR's David Greene, https://news.wbhm.org/npr_story_post/2015/chrissie-hynde-im-just-telling-my-story/.
3. Larry Butler, personal correspondence with author, October 2015.

ONE

1. Tim Lewis, "Chrissie Hynde: 'I never found life in music harder because I'm a woman,'" *The Guardian*, May 25, 2014, www.theguardian.com/music/2014/may/25/chrissie-hynde-interview-never-found-music-harder-because-woman.
2. "Jackie Wilson Biography," on Jackie Wilson Lover blog, https://jackiewilsonlover.wordpress.com/jackie-wilson-bio/.
3. Unattributed quotes are from Chrissie Hynde's memoir *Reckless*.
4. *Akron Beacon Journal*, obituary for Delores (Roberts) Hynde, November 6, 2012, www.legacy.com/obituaries/ohio/obituary.aspx?pid=160897365.
5. WTF with Marc Maron (podcast), "Chrissie Hynde," www.wtfpod.com/podcast/episodes/episode_556_-_chrissie_hynde.
6. Ibid.
7. Kurt Loder, "The Pretenders Ain't Sobbing," *Rolling Stone*, May 29, 1980, www.rollingstone.com/music/features/pretenders-19800529.

8. James McNair, "Q&A: Chrissie Hynde," *Team Rock*, May 9, 2014, www.teamrock.com/features/2014-05-09/q-a-chrissie-hynde.

9. "Pretenders Accept Award: Rock and Roll Hall of Fame Inductions 2005," YouTube video, www.youtube.com/watch?v =TQI4qCv8nls.

10. Paul Zollo, "Chrissie Hynde: The Bluerailroad Interview," *Bluerailroad*, n.d., https://bluerailroad.wordpress.com/chrissie -hynde-the-bluerailroad-interview/.

11. John Lydon, with Keith and Kent Zimmerman, *Rotten: No Irish, No Blacks, No Dogs* (New York: Picador, 2008).

12. "Hynde Sight," *Spin* 2, no. 9, December 1986.

13. Jon Savage, *The England's Dreaming Tapes* (Minneapolis: University of Minnesota Press, 2010).

14. Ibid.

15. Ibid.

16. Ibid.

17. Lydon, *Rotten*, 84.

18. Ibid.

19. "Confessions of an Anti-Christ: John Lydon in the Q Interview." *Q Magazine*, March 1992.

20. "'Way to Go, Ohio': Arthur's exclusive Q&A with the Pretenders' Chrissie Hynde and James Walbourne," *Arthur* magazine, December 2008, http://arthurmag.com/2008/12/17/pretenders-qa/.

21. Coincidentally, the date of the Pretenders' first gig in London, February 2, 1979, was also the day Sid Vicious died in New York City. She was very anxious before the show: "It's all the more nerve-racking, hometown gigs, when you have to deliver to people you actually know." In order not to rattle her further, her bandmates agreed to withhold the news of Sid's death from her until after their set, but someone else in the club told her about it just before they took the stage. She brought the shock up there with her. The Pretenders played what she called a "raggedy version" of the Troggs' "I Can't Control Myself" in his honor.

22. "The Kids Think Us Old Sods Are Cool," *Cambridge News*, October 5, 2006, www.cambridge-news.co.uk/kids-think-old-sods -cool/story-22773945-detail/story.html.

23. Viv Albertine, *Clothes, Clothes, Clothes. Music, Music, Music. Boys, Boys, Boys* (New York: Thomas Dunne, 2014).

24. Loder, "Pretenders Ain't Sobbing."

25. Savage, *England's Dreaming Tapes*.

26. Loder, "Pretenders Ain't Sobbing."

27. Zollo, "Chrissie Hynde: The Bluerailroad Interview."

28. "Chrissie Hynde Speaks Her Mind at the Airport: The Pretenders," YouTube video, www.youtube.com/watch?v=xzUyACTkdfo.

29. "Hynde Sight," *Spin*.

30. Robert Christgau, *Christgau's Record Guide: The '80s* (Boston: Da Capo Press, 1994).

31. "The Pretenders," Johnny Marr Plays Guitar website, www .johnnymarrplaysguitar.com/a-long-list-2/the-pretenders/.

32. Loder, "Pretenders Ain't Sobbing."

33. "Hynde Sight," *Spin*.

34. Mitch Easter, personal interview, January 2016.

CHAPTER TWO

1. *Outlandos* was a better and more important album than it may have seemed at the time. Though it was roasted by critics, it consummated a marriage of London's two main musical forces, reggae/ska and punk, with a pop ring.

2. In *Reckless*, Hynde recalls that the Pretenders and Van Halen appeared on the same German TV show a couple of years later. Jimmy Scott and Eddie Van Halen bored their bandmates geeking out on guitars; an arranged midnight jam session went by the boards after Scott passed out drunk.

3. Scott Miller, *Music: What Happened?* (N.p.: 125 Records, 2010).

4. Sasha Frere-Jones, "The Skeptic: Chrissie Hynde's Rock-and-Roll Sneer," *The New Yorker*, June 23, 2014, www.newyorker.com /magazine/2014/06/23/the-skeptic.

5. Kurt Loder, "The Pretenders Ain't Sobbing," *Rolling Stone*, May 29, 1980, www.rollingstone.com/music/features/pretenders -19800529.

6. Ibid.

7. "The Pretenders' James Honeyman-Scott." *Guitar Player*, April 1981.

8. Paul Zollo, "Chrissie Hynde: The Bluerailroad Interview," *Bluerailroad*, n.d., https://bluerailroad.wordpress.com/chrissie -hynde-the-bluerailroad-interview/.

9. WTF with Marc Maron (podcast), "Chrissie Hynde," www
.wtfpod.com/podcast/episodes/episode_556_-_chrissie_hynde.

10. "Chrissie Hynde Q&A," *Details*, March 1996.

11. *Akron Beacon Journal*, obituary for Delores (Roberts) Hynde,
November 6, 2012, www.legacy.com/obituaries/ohio/obituary.
aspx?pid=160897365.

CHAPTER THREE

1. Paul Zollo, "Chrissie Hynde: The Bluerailroad Interview,"
Bluerailroad, n.d., https://bluerailroad.wordpress.com/chrissie
-hynde-the-bluerailroad-interview/.

2. "Pretenders: Talk of the Town: Acoustic," YouTube video,
www.youtube.com/watch?v=N7Qb3_WX5TQ.

3. "Spoke to 'eem" is what she actually says, in her funny idiolect, a
patois of flat Midwestern, secondhand Brit, and tough-talking street-
rocker. Her vocabulary has long been sprinkled with Anglicisms:
"took the piss out of it," "get her kit off," "we didn't rate them."

4. "Pretenders: Talk of the Town: Acoustic," YouTube video,
www.youtube.com/watch?v=N7Qb3_WX5TQ.

5. Ibid.

6. She wants her bandmates to look that way, too. She told *Arthur*
magazine that throughout the lifespan of the Pretenders she has cho-
sen players partly (though not primarily) according to whether they
looked like Pretenders to her. They had to have the togs and the swag;
the guy playing guitar next to her had to be able to get the chicks she
was luring to the show.

7. David Gallant, "How I Got Started . . . Chrissie Hynde—Reckless
Rebel," *Guitar & Bass*, December 8, 2015, www.guitar-bass.net
/interviews/how-i-got-started-chrissie-hynde-reckless-rebel/.

8. James McNair, "Q&A: Chrissie Hynde," *Team Rock*, May 9, 2014,
www.teamrock.com/features/2014-05-09/q-a-chrissie-hynde.

9. "Chrissie Hynde's Advice to Chick Rockers," reproduced at
http://dangerousminds.net/comments/chrissie_hyndes_advice_to
_chick_rockers.

10. Wayne Fontana and the Mindbenders, "The Game of Love,"
on *The Game of Love*, Fontana Records, 1965.

11. *New Musical Express*, June 1974.

12. Scott Miller, *Music: What Happened?* (N.p.: 125 Records, 2010).

13. David Harding, "Chrissie Hynde Says She Smoked Pot with Tennis Star John McEnroe," *New York Daily News*, August 3, 2014, www.nydailynews.com/entertainment/gossip/chrissie-hynde-smoked-pot-john-mcenroe-article-1.1890298

14. Found at Trove, a website of the National Library of Australia: http://trove.nla.gov.au/work/99644653?q&versionId=113012746.

15. "Pretenders Accept Award: Rock and Roll Hall of Fame Inductions 2005," YouTube video, www.youtube.com/watch?v=TQI4qCv8nls.

CHAPTER FOUR

1. "Ray Davies," *People* 28 (no. 1), July 6, 1987.

2. Ray Davies, *Americana: The Kinks, the Riff, the Road: The Story* (New York: Sterling, 2013), 133.

3. Ray Davies, "Observations: Ray Davies' Ode to Icons of London," *Independent*, December 10, 2009, www.independent.co.uk/arts-entertainment/music/features/observations-ray-davies-ode-to-icons-of-london-1837702.html.

4. James Henke, "Chrissie Hynde without Tears." *Rolling Stone*, RS 420, April 26, 1984.

5. Ibid.

6. "Ray Davies," *People* 28 (no. 1), July 6, 1987.

7. The Pretenders, *Pirate Radio* booklet, Rhino Records, 2006.

8. Chambers wrote some material that was intended for the album but was never recorded.

9. Richard Buskin, "Classic Tracks: The Pretenders: Back on the Chain Gang," *Sound on Sound*, September 2005, www.soundonsound.com/sos/sep05/articles/classictracks.htm.

10. See www.songfacts.com/detail.php?id=1262.

11. Another disputed lyric: this word has also been rendered as both "past" and "plans," but actually sounds like "pants"—which, given her impending motherhood, does make a certain kind of sense. (So does the possibility that "pains" may refer to a life after labor pains.) Also, she fudges her age for the sake of a rhyme: "I'm not the cat [or kind] I used to be / I got a kid, I'm thirty-three," she snarls; in fact, she was thirty-two when she wrote the song.

12. Ray Davies, *Americana: The Kinks, The Riff, The Road: The Story* (New York: Sterling, 2013).

13. "Do Not Disturb," *Q Magazine*, June 1989.

14. Paul Zollo, "Chrissie Hynde: The Bluerailroad Interview," *Bluerailroad*, n.d., https://bluerailroad.wordpress.com/chrissie -hynde-the-bluerailroad-interview/.

15. IMDb, "The Breakfast Club (1985) Trivia," www.imdb.com/title /tt0088847/trivia.

CHAPTER FIVE

1. Chris Wade, "The Pretenders," *Hound Dawg* 6, April 2010 wisdomtwinsbooks.weebly.com/uploads/3/0/4/4/3044944/hound _dawg_6.pdf.

2. Ibid.

3. It wasn't the only time she gave another band a career boost. In 1981 she and Jimmy Scott heard the Violent Femmes busking in Milwaukee, where the Pretenders had a gig that night. She invited them to play a set after the Pretenders' show, netting the Femmes crucial exposure.

4. Scott Miller, *Music: What Happened?* (N.p.: 125 Records, 2010).

5. Kurt Loder, "The Pretenders Ain't Sobbing," *Rolling Stone*, May 29, 1980, www.rollingstone.com/music/features/pretenders -19800529.

6. *Billboard*, "Q&A with Chrissie Hynde," April 3, 2006, www .billboard.com/articles/news/58881/qa-with-chrissie-hynde.

7. "Chrissie Hynde's Advice to Chick Rockers," reproduced at http://dangerousminds.net/comments/chrissie_hyndes_advice_to _chick_rockers.

8. Robert Christgau, "Call the Doctor," *Village Voice*, June 6, 1999, http://robertchristgau.com/xg/rock/pretende-99.php.

9. She gave it a go anyway, starring in a short but slickly produced film that was contrived as the video for "Don't Get Me Wrong" but has nothing whatsoever to do with the song. The only other Pretender to appear, McIntosh, is on screen for about five seconds. She also did the usual lip-sync with the full band, temporarily a quintet, in the well-decorated videos for "My Baby" and "Hymn to Her."

10. 99.1 PLR (radio station), "This Day in Music History: June 8," www.wplr.com/this-day-in-music-history/2015/06/08/this-day-in -music-history-june-8th.

11. Associated Press, "Rock Singer Promises No More

Firebomb Jokes," June 13, 1989, www.apnewsarchive.com /1989/Rock-Singer-Promises-No-More-Firebomb-Jokes/id -0ae00488c0a95815a3feeb61b714b2a0.

12. *Salt Lake City Weekly's Daily Feed*, "I'm Hatin' It," August 22, 2009, www.cityweekly.net/TheDailyFeed/archives/2009/08/22/im -hatin-it.

13. "The Pretenders," Johnny Marr Plays Guitar website, www.johnnymarrplaysguitar.com/a-long-list-2/the-pretenders/.

14. "Rock's Greatest Pretender: Claire Prentice Meets a Mellow Chrissie Hynde," on the Pretenders Archives website, www .pretendersarchives.com/news/chhogmanayinterview.html.

15. WTF with Marc Maron (podcast), "Chrissie Hynde," www.wtfpod.com/podcast/episodes/episode_556_-_chrissie_hynde.

16. Tim Burrows, "Sarah Cracknell on Her Daily Routine, Touring and Her Love of Birds," *The Telegraph*, December 12, 2012, www .telegraph.co.uk/culture/music/9724090/Sarah-Cracknell-on-her -daily-routine-touring-and-her-love-of-birds.html.

CHAPTER SIX

1. Tim Lewis, "Chrissie Hynde: I Never Found Life in Music Harder because I Was a Woman," *The Guardian*, May 25, 2014, www .theguardian.com/music/2014/may/25/chrissie-hynde-interview -never-found-music-harder-because-woman.

2. Paul Zollo, "Chrissie Hynde: The Bluerailroad Interview," *Bluerailroad*, n.d., https://bluerailroad.wordpress.com/chrissie -hynde-the-bluerailroad-interview/.

3. On Songfacts, www.songfacts.com/detail.php?id=3736.

4. Zollo, "Chrissie Hynde: The Bluerailroad Interview."

5. Robert Christgau, "Pretenders," www.robertchristgau.com /get_artist.php?name=pretenders.

6. Alan Light, "Her City's Not Gone, and Neither Is She," *New York Times*, October 3, 2008, www.nytimes.com/2008/10/05/arts/music /05ligh.html?pagewanted=print&_r=0.

7. Charles Aaron, "Kim Deal: Breeders Leader Gets Pissed," *Spin* 11 (no. 4), July 1995.

8. "Chrissie's Wedding a Right Pizza-Up," *The Mirror*, July 11, 1997.

9. Chris Rilegh, "Stoners We Love: Chrissie Hynde," *Daily Joint*, August 6, 2014, www.dailyjoint.com/stoners-we-love-chrissie-hynde/.

10. Robert Christgau, "Call the Doctor," *Village Voice*, June 6, 1999, http://robertchristgau.com/xg/rock/pretende-99.php.

11. Rilegh, "Stoners."

12. WTF with Marc Maron (podcast), "Chrissie Hynde," www.wtfpod.com/podcast/episodes/episode_556_-_chrissie_hynde.

13. See, for example, Lewis, "Chrissie Hynde."

14. Ibid.

15. Christgau, "Call the Doctor."

16. "Chrissie Hynde a Kinky Role Model and She's Not about to Soften Up For," *Newsday*, June 19, 1999, www.newsday.com /entertainment/2.828/chrissie-hynde-a-kinky-role-model-and -she-s-not-about-to-soften-up-for-1.467307

17. Ibid.

18. Ibid.

19. "Chrissie Hynde: Samurai—Bs. As., 13/11/04," YouTube video, www.youtube.com/watch?v=O—LwDE0T1o

20. Many of Chrissie Hynde's musical descendants not only paid tribute but did so publicly. Shirley Manson, the lead singer of Garbage, was a longtime fan. She interpolated the line "we were the talk of the town" into Garbage's song, "Special"—the title itself an echo of the talismanic word in "Brass in Pocket." Under pressure from her litigation-fearing label to remove the line, Manson sent her heroine a request for permission to include it. The very next day, a fax arrived that read, according to Manson: "I, Chrissie Hynde, hereby allow Garbage, the rock band, to sample any of my sounds, my voice, or indeed my very ass" (www.pretendersarchives.com/Qanda.html#Garbage). She asked for neither credit nor royalties.

21. On the MusiMapp website: http://worldonmusic.com/tag/silvio -rodriguez/.

22. More deception: *rabo* means "tail," but it's also slang for "penis."

CHAPTER SEVEN

1. Steven J. Rosen, *Holy Cow: The Hare Krishna Contribution to Vegetarianism* (New York: Lantern, 2004).

2. Paul Zollo, "Chrissie Hynde: The Bluerailroad Interview," *Bluerailroad*, n.d., https://bluerailroad.wordpress.com/chrissie -hynde-the-bluerailroad-interview/.

3. Greg Kot, "Hynde Frolics in Plain Sight: Pretenders

Frontwoman Follows Her Busy Muse," *Chicago Tribune*, February 7, 2003, http://articles.chicagotribune.com/2003-02-07/entertainment /0302070400_1_pretenders-loose-screw-chrissie-hynde.

4. Robert Christgau, "Call the Doctor," *Village Voice*, June 6, 1999, http://robertchristgau.com/xg/rock/pretende-99.php.

5. All of the Goldberg quotes are from a telephone interview with the author, October 2015.

6. Tim Masters, "Pretenders' Rockabilly Return," *BBC News*, http://news.bbc.co.uk/2/hi/entertainment/8070423.stm.

7. The Rush Limbaugh Show, "Origins of the EIB Theme Song," May 13, 2011, www.rushlimbaugh.com/daily/2011/05/13/origins_of _the_eib_theme_song.

8. Alan Sculley, "Interview: Pretenders Drummer Martin Chambers," Nuvo.net, February 3, 2009, www.nuvo.net/indianapolis /pretenders-martin-chambers-lets-loose/Content?oid=1271267.

9. Sasha Frere-Jones, "The Skeptic: Chrissie Hynde's Rock-and-Roll Sneer," *The New Yorker*, June 23, 2014, www.newyorker.com /magazine/2014/06/23/the-skeptic.

10. Sculley, "Interview."

CHAPTER EIGHT

1. Whitney Matheson, "Chrissie Hynde Is Inspired by New Love— and Vampires," *USA Today*, August 19, 2010, http://content.usatoday .com/communities/popcandy/post/2010/08/chrissie-hynde-is -inspired-by-new-love——and-vampires-/1#.VtcTIpwrKUk.

2. Nathan Bevan, "Great Pretender Chrissie Hynde on Her Harmony with Young Welsh Singer JP Jones," *Wales Online*, March 28, 2013, www.walesonline.co.uk/news/wales-news/great-pretender -chrissie-hynde-harmony-1891782.

3. Adrian Mack, "JP, Chrissie, and the Fairground Boys Have More than Just Luck," *The Georgia Straight*, October 13, 2010, www.straight .com/article-352512/vancouver/more-just-fairground-luck.

4. WTF with Marc Maron (podcast), "Chrissie Hynde," www.wtfpod.com/podcast/episodes/episode_556_-_chrissie_hynde.

5. Falling James, "'I'm Not so Hateful as I Used to Be': The Pretenders' Chrissie Hynde and Former Lover J. P. Jones Discuss New Band JP, Chrissie, and the Fairground Boys," *LA Weekly*, August 20, 2010, www.laweekly.com/music/im-not-so-hateful-as-i-used-to-be

-the-pretenders-chrissie-hynde-and-former-lover-jp-jones-discuss
-new-band-jp-chrissie-and-the-fairground-boys-2406144.

6. "Even today, she claims not to know which Pretenders songs have been licensed for commercial use." Sasha Frere-Jones, "The Skeptic: Chrissie Hynde's Rock-and-Roll Sneer," *The New Yorker*, June 23, 2014, www.newyorker.com/magazine/2014/06/23/the-skeptic.

7. "Chrissie Hynde Steps Out, but She's Not Alone," *All Things Considered*, July 12, 2014, www.npr.org/2014/07/12/329867867/chrissie -hynde-steps-out-but-shes-not-alone.

8. Ibid.

9. Status update on Lucinda Williams's Facebook page: www.facebook.com/LucindaWilliams/posts/10153646774809189

10. David Greene, "Chrissie Hynde: 'I'm Just Telling My Story,'" *Morning Edition*, October 6, 2015, www.npr.org/2015/10/06/446083413 /chrissie-hynde-im-just-telling-my-story.

180

SELECTED DISCOGRAPHY

***PRETENDERS* (SIRE, 1980)**

If you buy only one Pretenders album, it has to be this one. What's re-markable is how quickly it metamorphoses from punk to pop, and by the end has moved through reggae and soul: the band is in time-lapse evolution, without a single second of self-doubt in forty-seven min-utes of music. It's one of the clearest examples of its time of what the mainstream could do with punk without losing punk's spirit.

***PRETENDERS II* (SIRE, 1981)**

The worrying thing about a great debut is that it might be a fluke, but "Talk of the Town" alone dispels that concern—and the band is kind enough to provide a whole LP's worth of reassurance. It's not as great as *Pretenders*, but *Pretenders II* offers more than enough evidence that this band is legitimate. Side one opens with the rollicking trio of "The Adultress," "Bad Boys Get Spanked," and "Message of Love," then follows those with the gorgeous "Birds of Paradise." On side two the mood gets heavier, and James Honeyman-Scott serves stronger notice—terribly sad in retrospect—that he was probably on his way to becoming a guitar great.

SELECTED DISCOGRAPHY

LEARNING TO CRAWL (SIRE, 1984)
Less a comeback than a double-reinvention—of the band, and of Chrissie Hynde's persona. This is what the big early eighties sounded like right before they went over the edge. It's an apotheosis, a classic, and the last great Pretenders album. "Time the Avenger" and "Show Me" are two of her most undervalued songs. It's always a good sign when the track on an album you most readily skip is its cover song.

GET CLOSE (SIRE/WEA, 1986)
Blame the eighties, blame motherhood, blame the players, blame the loss of Chris Thomas—but Chrissie Hynde herself sings the real reason that this is the Pretenders' worst album: "If there's a method to writing a song, how come I'm getting it wrong?" Buy "Don't Get Me Wrong" if you must and leave the LP to the cut-out bins. Amy Winehouse could have shot "Chill Factor" to the moon.

PACKED! (SIRE/WEA, 1990)
Although Robert Christgau seemed crazy to give this modest album an A-minus grade when it came out, it's by no means the dud Chrissie Hynde called it. Even the Rhino Records reissue liner notes conceded that *Packed!* "may not be the best offering ever to emerge under the Pretenders' name." It's nonetheless a perfectly respectable placeholder—but as none other than Ray Davies said in his Hall of Fame induction speech on behalf of the Kinks, "Rock and roll has become respectable. What a bummer." The reggae tune "How Do I Miss You" will sneak up on you if you aren't careful.

LAST OF THE INDEPENDENTS (SIRE/WEA, 1994)
The title is a lie, so are a number of the songs, and the album still has that unpleasant eighties gloss on it. It has better songs and sound than its eighties forbear, *Get Close*, but it's ultimately less tolerable. Its naked commercial ambition makes it both more aggressive and less sincere: Hollywood perfume, as the lead track's title indicates. It's also less tolerable because it led to Rod Stewart's execrable cover of "I'll Stand by You." To quote that schmaltz, if you're mad, get mad—but it got her back in the chain stores.

THE ISLE OF VIEW (WARNER BROS., 1995)

Chances are you'll want to like this more than you actually do. The idea of throwing a live string quartet at Pretenders songs is intriguing, but the Duke Quartet is underused, and the arrangements (by their violist, John Metcalfe) are mostly wallpaper. They drag the songs out too long and bloat the entire sluggish affair to a listless hour, including a silly version of "The Phone Call." It's too bad the Pretenders' version of Radiohead's "Creep," recorded at the same time, isn't included. Still, "Revolution" is nearly rescued by the string treatment, and the new Pretenders, Andy Hobson and Adam Seymour, will stand their leader in good stead going forward.

¡VIVA EL AMOR! (WARNER BROS., 1999)

The true Pretenders comeback album. In a just world it would have sold better and put the band back in the mainstream, but instead it was DOA thanks mostly to Warner's lack of marketing interest. That neglect leaves the album to stand entirely on its own merits, which it quite stoutly does. It's fun to hear Chrissie Hynde egg on Jeff Beck during his solo in "Legalise Me." This is the last album that purveys the Pretenders Guitar Sound.

LOOSE SCREW (ARTEMIS, 2002)

New Yorker critic Sasha Frere-Jones claimed that *Loose Screw* "should have made Hynde more famous, more respected" (although its predecessor *¡Viva El Amor!* should already have accomplished that). It's great-sounding, catchy, emotive, expansive, and assured. But in retrospect, it sounds less like the next heavyweight Pretenders album and more like Chrissie Hynde's transition out of the band altogether, thanks mainly to the heavy dose of high-gloss post-reggae that seems to have an indirect kinship with the Brazilian music she got into soon after *Loose Screw* had run its quiet, noncommercial course.

PIRATE RADIO (RHINO, 2006)

This four-disc compilation is all you need if you want an overview (there's no point in owning the 1987 *Singles* best-of), and it renders the Rhino reissues of much of the Pretenders catalog unnecessary, as well. It throws in a lot of extras, including a cover of her friend Morrissey's "Every Day Is Like Sunday," recorded just for the occasion. The other covers, demos, and live versions—including an entire DVD of the latter—are fun for aficionados, as are the extensive liner notes. More meaningful, perhaps, is the rescued-from-outtakes "Worlds within Worlds," a mid-eighties tune, angularly recorded, that offers a what-if alternate history of the Pretenders from around the time of *Get Close*: it's much better than most of that album's songs, but it didn't make the cut.

BREAK UP THE CONCRETE (SHANGRI-LA MUSIC, 2008)

Surprisingly affecting, and better if you don't think of it as a Pretenders album but rather as the sessions of a really good pickup band knocking out some tunes, all but one of which happen to be Chrissie Hynde's. The ramshackle performances and papery sound befit the proceedings. One thing she's seldom managed to do is sound relaxed, and here she sounds relaxed for the whole album. Rhyming "unemployable, illegal" with "you're a whole film by Don Siegel" adds a bonus point.

FIDELITY! (JP, CHRISSIE, AND THE FAIRGROUND BOYS; LA MINA/ROCKET SCIENCE VENTURES, 2010)

Passionate but ungrounded, *Fidelity!* doesn't withstand repeated listening. Chrissie Hynde hitched her star to JP Jones's wagon, but he wasn't the great songwriter she claimed. Though she spent a career singing mostly by herself, as a duettist she's formidable: pushy, tangy, gutsy. When she and Jones sing in harmony, the songs take off. He proves he can hang with her vocally, but as an unknown sharing billing with a legend, his musical presence is otherwise inert; so, alas, is *Fidelity!* If only she'd made an album with a more viable partner, like Jeff Tweedy or even Ben Folds.

STOCKHOLM (CHRISSIE HYNDE; CAROLINE, 2014)

Leonard Cohen took Berlin on *I'm Your Man*; here Chrissie Hynde takes Stockholm—its Europop, its weltschmerz, its *chanteuse* tradition—and she does it with a vocal range that is low and limited like Cohen's, while barely appearing to move a muscle in effort. Yet *Stockholm* undeniably works on its own terms. It's an album only fans of hers will generally bother seeking out, but it has a good chance to hold up well over the years, John McEnroe's lame guitar cameo notwithstanding. Something about the odd if/then rhetorical construction of the lyrics to "In a Miracle" is opaquely mystical.

INDEX

adolescence of, 6–11; compositional approach of, 37–38, 54,
63, 78, 89, 96–97, 116, 131, 159;
drug use by, 7–8, 12–13, 18, 64,
68, 122, 131; fashion and style of,
59–61, 174; feminism of, 92–95,
164–165; forming the Pretenders, 24–26, 28–32; motherhood
and, 69, 75, 87–88, 98–99,
105–106; musical influences
on, 6–10, 14, 25, 42; persona/
character/public perception of,
1–3, 8, 26–28, 65, 74–75, 120–121,
141–142, 144, 153, 170–171; and
punk rock, 17, 20–23; spirituality of, 138–141; work habits of,
122–123
Hynde, Dolores, 9, 23, 50, 144
Hynde, Natalie, 74, 85–87
Hynde, Terry, 9, 95, 150, 160

Idol, Billy, 87
"I Go to Sleep," 63–64
"I Got You Babe," 90
"I Hurt You," 85
"I'll Stand by You," 116, 119, 121,
130, 157, 182
"I'm a Mother," 39, 94, 119
"In a Miracle," 184
Iovine, Jimmy, 89
"I Should Of," 136
Isle of View, The, 70, 119, 183

Jack Rabbit, 18–19, 24, 103, 156
Jackson, Janet, 97
Jackson, Michael, 65, 92
"Jealous Dogs," 66–67, 94
Jefferson Starship, 91
Jett, Joan, 61
Johansen, David, 127

Jones, Brian, 7
Jones, Grace, 48, 164
Jones, JP, 154–157, 158, 159, 184
Jones, Rickie Lee, 142
Jones, Steve, 17
JP, Chrissie, and the Fairground
Boys, 155–156

Katydids, the, 117
Kaye, Lenny, 58
Keene, Meg, 5, 92
Kelly, Tom, 115–118, 121, 127–130,
134
Keltner, Jim, 146
Kensit, Patsy, 65, 127
Kent, Nick, 16–17, 117–118
Kent State University, 8, 9, 12–15, 95
Kerr, Jim, 65, 86–88, 99, 113, 122,
127, 154, 163
Kerr, Yasmin, 87–88
"Kid," 30, 47–48, 50, 81, 94, 118, 155
Kidney, Robert, 149
Kilmister, Lemmy, 24–25, 29, 153
"Kinda Nice, I Like It," 135–136
Kingsmen, the, 67
Kinks, the, 8, 30, 63, 74–76, 182

"Labour of Love," 72, 76
Last of the Independents, 39, 93,
115–119, 182
"Last Ride, The," 148, 149
Laughner, Peter, 18
Lauper, Cyndi, 97, 116
Learning to Crawl, 10, 72–88, 90, 96,
100, 136, 150, 182
"Legalise Me," 82, 131–132, 138, 150,
158, 183
Lennon, John, 27
Lennox, Annie, 122
"Let's Make a Pact," 102

INDEX